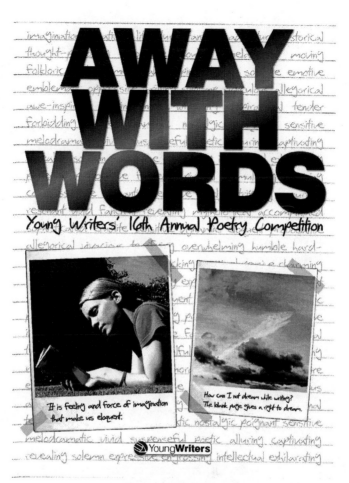

AWAY WITH WORDS

Young Writers' 16th Annual Poetry Competition

How can I not dream while writing?
The blank page gives a right to dream.

It is feeling and force of imagination
that make us eloquent.

Kent Verses

Edited by Michelle Afford

 Young**Writers**

First published in Great Britain in 2007 by:
Young Writers
Remus House
Coltsfoot Drive
Peterborough
PE2 9JX
Telephone: 01733 890066
Website: www.youngwriters.co.uk

SB ISBN 978-1 84602 961 5

Contents

Astor College for the Arts
Kyra Sedgwick (13)   1

Babington House School
Rebecca Leharne (14)   2

Bennett Memorial Diocesan School
Nicholas Parkes (15)   3
Katrina Harper (16)   4
Jon Braund (15)   5
Sam Hooke (15)   6
Amy Sichel (11)   6
Rebecca Kemp (15)   7
Will Moore (15)   7
Jennifer Leafe (16)   8
Angela Cameron (15)   8
Emily Cammell (15)   9
Archie Carey (11)   9
Ben Cook (16)   10
Ellie Bland (15)   11
Rachel Bell (15)   12
Lauren Beeching (15)   12
Sophie Barnes (15)   13

Caldecott Foundation School
Paul Woodward (15)   14
John Knipe (13)   14
Sky Kerr (14)   15
Albert Webb (14)   16
Theresa Tysoe (14)   16
Dwayne Thomas (13)   17
Ryan Brannigan (14)   17

Cator Park School for Girls
Julianna Boateng (14)   18
Sarah Burns (14)   18
Simara John (14)   19
Mica Walters (14)   19

Kelly Walker (13)   20
Jessica Nettell (16)   21
Charlotte Fuller (12)   22
Hermione Salmon (16)   23
Millie Hayes (13)   24
Laura Walton (13)   25
Julia Margetts (11)   26
Louisa Burrows (12)   27
Esme Tyler (13)   28
Rachel Tracey (15)   29

Cleeve Park School
Lucy Shirley Paine (13)   29
Joe Drake (13)   30
Harry Green (11)   30
Joshua Bowers (12)   31
Rebecca Cox (13)   31
Amy Dunn (12)   31
Pius Inebode (12)   32
Rachel Brackpool (12)   32
Ib Onarinde (12)   33
Scott Best (12)   33
Jamilia Sooh (11)   34
Scott Merkell (12)   34
Darius Groeger (13)   35
Michelle Zviripayi (13)   35
Matthew Higgs (11)   36
Danni Rouse (11)   36
Louise Smith   37
Shyan Sittampalam (12)   38
Phillip White (13)   38
James Rogers (11)   38
James Arsmtrong (13)   39
Shaun Brown (11)   39
Tobie Mitchell (13)   39
Amy O'Connor (11)   40
Faye Donohoe (11)   40
Tom Moore (11)   41
Cameron Terry (13)   41

Combe Bank School
Scarlett Chapman (14)   42

Dartford Grammar School for Girls
Yuk Yee Vuong (12)   43
Infanta Suganthanaikabahu (12)   44
Olivia Searle (13)   45
Rachel Long (18)   46
Abbie Noakes (13)   47
Charlotte Sloan (12)   48
Lydia Caplan (13)   49
Jody Bloom (14)   49

Dover College
Emily Howkins (13)   50
Sam Hubbard (13)   51
Tom Robson (13)   52
Josh Corney (13)   52
Peter Vickerman (14)   53
Chandy Castle (14)   53
Richard Bowen (14)   54
Jack Hennessey (13)   54
Amy Rollinson (14)   55

Glyne Gap School
Kyile White & Louise Godin (15)   56

Gravesend Grammar School for Boys
Sam Mattacott (15)   56
Robert Humphries (14)   57
Matthew Blakemore (15)   57
Nicholas Wilson (14)   58
Darren Horner (14)   59
Tom Harper (15)   60
Danny Payne (14)   60
Ricky Dhami (14)   61
Connor O'Flynn (14)   61
James Simmons (15)   62
Jonathan Beresford (15)   63
Robb Henderson (15)   64

Thomas Saunders (15)	65
Brendan Johnson (14)	66
Jonathan Foster (15)	67
Sean Walsh (14)	68
Kyle Ludlow (15)	69
Manbir Mand (15)	70

Harbour School

Victoria Ross (15)	70
Caroline Piercey (14)	71
Rhys Mitchell (15)	71
Paul Leatham (14)	72
Josie Mockett (15)	72
Gemma Chapman (14)	73
Ivan Hunter-Johnson (15)	73
Sasha Smith (15)	74

Herne Bay High School

Kacie Hawkins (12)	74
Lauren Hopkins (11)	75
Jasmine Thomas (11)	75
Fred Pearce (13)	76
Joshua Walton (13)	76
Sadie Williams (14)	77
Jamie Robertson (12)	77
Naomi Hougham (14)	78
Hannah Plail (12)	79
Hannah Sheppard (13)	80
Callum Mason-Decker (13)	80
Anthony Benge (12)	81
Charlotte Guilliard (14)	82
James Dean (11)	82
Natasha Savage (14)	83
Megan Catling (12)	84
Leonie Hopkins (14)	84
Rebecca Arnold (14)	85
Stacey Norris (14)	85
Jack Davey (13)	86
Shanon-Kate Woolls (13)	86
Freddie Mills (11)	87
Bethany Guilliard (11)	87

Shannen Hildred (12)	88
Abi Hollingsbee-Pert (14)	88
Charlotte Hiles (12)	89
Rebecca Smith (12)	89
Sophie Collins (11)	90
Lucia Wheeler (12)	90
Kerry Maeers (11)	91
Ben Critchley (13)	91
Emily Reynolds (11)	92
Oliver Whiting (12)	92
Grace Franklin (11)	93
Emma Hunter (12)	93
Tia Hills (12)	94
Ellie Surridge (11)	94
Ashley Hoskins (12)	95
Georgina Lambert (12)	95
Sarah Kyte (12)	96
Victoria Lawrence (12)	96
Mollie Eyles (11)	97
Jake Heddershaw (12)	97
Adam Ford (12)	98
Ashley Nevard (11)	98
Matt Radley (12)	99
Sarah McCracken (11)	99
Chenelle Williams (12)	100
Ryan Cubbage (11)	100
Jason Chow (12)	101
Luke Corrigan (12)	101
Sam Sinclair (12)	102
Katie Packman (12)	102
Nadia Commentucci (12)	103
Abigail Heard (11)	103
Katie Gurney (13)	104
Ben Hughes (11)	105
Kerrie Anderson (12)	105
Thomas Wickens (12)	106
Clare Bates (13)	106
Lauren Snoad (13)	107

King Ethelbert School

Tanya Stevens (12)	107
Craig Barsby (15)	108
Shane Gonesh (12)	108
Lauren Harris (15)	109
Ebony Barkes (12)	109
Emma Baggus (14)	110
Emma Kerr (13)	111
Emily Jeffries (12)	111
Franchesca Onken (12)	112
Joshua Lee (13)	112

St Anthony's School, Margate

Carl Harris (15)	113
Robert Reynolds (15)	113
Bret Linsdell (14)	114

St Edmund's Catholic School, Dover

Jonathan & Michael Hanly (18)	114
Daniel Sims (15)	115

Simon Langton Boys' School

Tim Benfield (12)	115

Tonbridge Grammar School

Anna Chadwick (11)	116
Mari Shirley (11)	117
Charlotte Whittaker (12)	118
Rachel Hannah (11)	119
Alice Hill (11)	120
Amie Humphrey (12)	121
Rebecca Fox (11)	122
Amy-Jane Greenwood (12)	122
Megan Beddoe (11)	123
Laura Morrison (11)	123
Eleanor Horswill (11)	124
Samantha Stephenson (12)	124
Joanna Barnett (12)	125
Emma Keywood (12)	126
Emma Beale (12)	127

Alice Matthews (11)   128
Alex St Clair (12)   129
Tilly Leeper (12)   130
Martha Jesson (11)   131
Jasmine Vorley (12)   132
Jemima Silver (12)   133
Lydia Hamblet (11)   134
Katie Pembroke (12)   134

Walthamstow Hall School

Alexandra Baddeley (12)   135

The Poems

Child Abuse

I was home alone
With my teddy called Frown
Sitting in the corner
Crying for help.

My mummy and daddy came walking in
Shouting and swearing, 'Where have you been?'
They hit me and bruised me all over my body
Shouting, 'Why are you here?'

They locked me away for a couple of days
No food, no drink, no light.
I could hear them fighting and my mummy screaming
She came running in with a knife
Not realising I was standing behind her
With my teddy in my hands.

My mummy knocked me over
I never saw the bedroom door again.

Kyra Sedgwick (13)
Astor College for the Arts

Changing Worlds

The plane touches down,
Wheels hissing on the wet tarmac,
The new country looms in the fog,
Through the window I see many things,
Yellow taxis with smoking lights,
A cold city so dull and grey
Hard buildings leering up out of the smog.

We climb into a yellow taxi and off we go,
Past grey buildings, grey faces,
Battling against the wind,
The only colour comes from the traffic lights,
After an hour we stop outside a block of flats
We walk up many flights of stairs
The television's blaring from behind the peeling green door
This is our only comfort, that something other than rats live here.

On the top floor is our flat
We open the door to find a large room - one of four
My bedroom is the smallest with a view over the harbour
The smell of fish is caught in the wind
Blowing itself into my bedroom
As evening falls over the city
Enough lights to light a country come on and buildings are alight
Blazing in the dark like fireflies.

Rebecca Leharne (14)
Babington House School

My Never-Ending Story (As The Crowd Roars)

As the beat starts, the stage is yours
Straight in with friends alongside
All dancing to the same beat.

Someone trying to steal your moves
Make you trip and fall
Ha-ha, no way
Dip it low, bring it back
And oh, too fast for you
You're gonna lose it all today.

But noooo! Crash and burn, that was too harsh, too bad
Pick up the pieces, pull it all back, start again and improvise.
As you finish you have to realise that it was all just a moment
Just your five minutes of fame in a never-ending story
Five minutes of trying to make yourself heard
A hundred people deciding your future
A hundred people to say yes or no.

Win or lose, it's not for you to say
As you walk away
Just a man again
Nothing ever matters
It's always back to the same beats
The same streets.

It's my never-ending story.

Nicholas Parkes (15)
Bennett Memorial Diocesan School

The Wings

The darkness is my comfort zone,
It's cosy and safe,
The inky black is like a mother bird cradling her chicks.

Outside the nest;
It's bright, exposed, fast-moving, action-packed and big,
That's not my comfort zone
But I've got to go.

Going on the stage is like being kicked out the nest,
I'm either going to fly or crash.

If it goes right I'll be soaring, weaving, gliding
I'll feel total euphoria . . .
If it goes wrong I'll be the fledgling bird
The one no one wants to know
The 'ugly duckling'.

The audience are the judges,
If I glide I will be the golden eagle,
The one people will wait hours for
Just to catch a glimpse.

If I crash, I'll be the dodo.
The extinct. 'Once upon a time . . .'
But no more.

1 . . . 2 . . . 3
My heart pounding
Mind racing
Hands shaking
It's time . . .

To fly or crash
Golden eagle or dodo
Gliding or falling . . .

Katrina Harper (16)
Bennett Memorial Diocesan School

Lost In Another World

Time for work again
Another day, the same old day
But there's a new thing each day
As you plug yourself in
Throw yourself into another world
The world of music.

Walking to work
Losing yourself in the song
Humming along
Singing along
Everything else a blur
The mood of the song reflected
In your face
Your walk,
Your actions.

The song reflects your life
It represents events in your past
What you want to happen
How you are feeling at present.

There are songs that remind you about
Being hurt
Losing everything, but also
Being happy
Having people around you
Living a life of excitement.

It gets to your favourite song
A dance anthem
But you're through the doors of work
So you unplug yourself
Thrown back into the real world.

Jon Braund (15)
Bennett Memorial Diocesan School

Dream Dance

I drift like a cloud;
swiftly, silently, vigorously
I twist and turn
like a leaf
in the storm of
the prancing
colours in
the subtle
guidance of
my dream
shaped by
the free-styling
wind of
opportunity
of downpour of
disappointment
the melody
slows, my
imagination
turns but
the pulse persists
rhyme, rhythm, pulse
first rays of light, the curtain opens.

Sam Hooke (15)
Bennett Memorial Diocesan School

Tree

Someone is throttling that tree
Being strangled, thrown and pushed
Branches waving around, being pushed in the darkness
Being pushed side to side
Roots holding in the ground
Waving, swaying and being rocked
Sighing and moaning falling to the ground.

Amy Sichel (11)
Bennett Memorial Diocesan School

Don't Save Me The Last Dance

B ase
E xcitement
A tmosphere
T wist

Life is my dance floor
Moving my way through
But it's the music I adore
Rock, pop, hip hop
My partners with me. All true.

As the disco ball shines
Reflecting the images of my past
My short life declines
Ballroom, tango, swing
As it travels so fast.

So don't save me the last dance
As I will not stop
But take my chance
Foxtrot, salsa, waltz
Until I drop!

Rebecca Kemp (15)
Bennett Memorial Diocesan School

Talent=Power=Greed

The glowing hubbub of the room filled with fans
Is silenced as he walks onto the stage.
When they realise it's him by his distinguished hair
Their faces fill with joy as they cheer.

The sound of his guitar sends the crowd wild
As if he is a god preaching the word to his followers.

And I think to myself that with this talent
he could raise up an army of supporters
But to have talent so great and wowing
Is to have power to change a nation's views.

Will Moore (15)
Bennett Memorial Diocesan School

My Final Ballet Lesson

Ballet is so graceful.
It pushes me.
I am forever holding on.
Holding on to those I care about
But soon I will need to let go,
Get on with my life.
The rhythm of the music pushes me,
As I reach up I am still holding on,
Gripping tightly,
I still have control,
I want to keep going
But it hurts.
It will be better for me to let go,
Holding,
Clutching,
Finally, I let myself free.

I am all alone now.

Jennifer Leafe (16)
Bennett Memorial Diocesan School

Waltz Me Once Again

Waltz me once again around the dance floor
Make my head go spinning round
As my head gets woozy
A blur of twinkling night lights pass.

Waltz me once again around the dance floor
My dress floating at my ankles
My hair bouncing to the beat of the waltz
Those were the young days . . .

Waltz me once again around the dance floor
Let the knees of frailness glide
Make it a finale never to forget
For it is the dance floor that will soon pass by.

Angela Cameron (15)
Bennett Memorial Diocesan School

The Dance Goes On

You asked me to dance
I said yes.
But I could never have guessed
How our individual beats
Would become one.

The stars shone above us
Our secret spotlight
Yet we danced through the night:
Fast . . . slow . . . fast again.

We matched and danced together as one.

My heart sped, the beat quickened,
Yet you calmed it with your soft melody.
We continued our dance to the break of day,
But the dream was soon to end.

The sun began to rise, the spotlights vanished,
The dream at an end, we had to part
But always, deep in my heart
The dance goes on . . .
The beat never stops.

Emily Cammell (15)
Bennett Memorial Diocesan School

I Like Noise

The whoop of a boy, the thud of a hoof
The rattle of rain on a galvanised roof.
The hubbub of traffic, the roar of a train
The throb of machinery numbing the brain.
The cry of a baby wanting her milk
The rustling of a dress made out of silk.
The sigh of the wind, the shout of a team
The noise of a police car straight to a scene.
I close my window and hop into bed
All I can hear is the noise in my head.

Archie Carey (11)
Bennett Memorial Diocesan School

Music Is A Personal Thing

Dance
The music hits my body like a trance
I'm fightin' to keep up
The beat is too fast
This dance may be my last
The music's like a story.

Break
It's all fake
R 'n' B
No subtlety.

Freestyle is what I like
Whether walking on the street
Or lyin' on my bed
Music is what makes me lose my head.

No matter where I am
No matter what I do
There is no right or wrong
There is no bad or good.

Music is a personal thing
It's what makes me happy when I'm down
I dance and move the way I like
Paying no attention to stare nor frown.

Ben Cook (16)
Bennett Memorial Diocesan School

A Dance Affair

Ditched
Torn apart . . . cast aside
A fist slams to the left
Echoes the rage that stings my disgusted soul
I fall to the floor, sudden, body collapsed
Echoes my crushed, crumpled spirit
Next dancer on; I skulk in the shadows
Of the stage, it's my life
As I wait, the image of them both joined as one blocks
                    all other thoughts
The taste of his kiss still lingering in my mouth
The smell of his breath still embedded in my hair
Envious, poisoned blood runs freely through my veins
The music changes, the lights go from green to white
I'm thrust on again, this time it's different
My movements lift my spirit
Leaps, jumps, I bound across the stage
I feel free
The audience clap and cheer with enthusiasm and passion
I feel wanted
I'm willing to move up . . . move on
He is nothing but a sheer distant memory
Accepted.

Ellie Bland (15)
Bennett Memorial Diocesan School

Life Is A Dance

Life is a dance and we move to its beat
The music carries us off our feet.
From the first steps as a child,
Discovering the stage; the world that surrounds you.

Moving through your teenage years
Freestyling - you just don't care.
The sequence you follow, has no form,
No one tells you what to do or how to dance.

But soon to grow up
And follow the sequence of life,
You move on to partners,
To dance 'until death do us part'.

Gradually, life goes on . . .
The melody slows
You realise your dance can't last forever . . .
It must come to an end.

Rachel Bell (15)
Bennett Memorial Diocesan School

Carnival

Listen, do you hear?

The tang of the steel drums, it pulses right through me,
From the tips of my fingers to the tips of my toes.
A ripple of envy, it wavers and falters
As I follow the steps as the dancers go.

Hips moving swift as the flow follows through
To the crowd, the flamenco, they dance to the sea
And the costumes, they flap like birds of paradise
Across on the sand, the carnival and me.

The people, the dances, the shimmering light,
The beautiful sunset, our silhouettes plain,
The music, the union, the rhythm, the night
I open my eyes and we dance through the rain.

Lauren Beeching (15)
Bennett Memorial Diocesan School

Exam Waltz

Checkerboard; the formation of the room
Each student at their square desk with paper and pen

One, two, three
One, two, three

There's a twisted rhythm of pen nibs scratching
And the flap of a page as it turns

One, two, three
One, two, three

Pulse of brainwaves; biology, physics, chemistry
The subtle choreography of the dance

One, two, three
One, two, three

The tap of heels on bare boards, echoed throughout the hall
Imagine the gentle sway of a lady's skirt

One, two, three
One, two, three

Sweep of the wrist and flap of cream-coloured satin as she moves
Ripple through the room as the waltz begins . . .

One, two, three
One, two, three.

Sophie Barnes (15)
Bennett Memorial Diocesan School

Horses

Neigh! The horses call to each other
As winter comes they all take cover
It's wet and cold, so they can't go in the field
If they do then they all have to shield
From the blistering winds that hurt their eyes.

When they see a human they all snort
They see the tack that she has brought
When they are all in the field they get caught.

Trotting along the brown damp sand
Holding the reins in her hand
Kicking her heels she canters along
The horse's hooves beating a song.

Tired and happy they both go home
The horse is sad now that he is alone
In his stable in the dead of the night
Snuffly noises in the quiet.

Paul Woodward (15)
Caldecott Foundation School

Out Of Breath

Just got up
Must warm up
Going for a run in the glorious sun
Getting hot but cannot stop
Must keep going till I drop.
Distance running by myself
I will keep going for my health
Sweating like mad and full of pain
Must keep going for the gain.
Getting thirsty, keep on going
Out of breath, near to death
Really thirsty, throat is dry
I just really want to cry.

John Knipe (13)
Caldecott Foundation School

The Deceit Of Love

Have you ever fallen in love
But they put you down
Divorcing or saying,
'You're dumped'?

Do they know
Your heart is breaking
Slowly?

You're happy with your life
It stops.

What are you going to do?
You want your life back on track.

Being friends is the hardest bit
Then they want you back
So what are you going to do?

Should you say yes?
Should you say no?

Have you ever fallen in love?
Have you ever had to choose?

The deceit of love
Have you made these
Decisions?

Sky Kerr (14)
Caldecott Foundation School

Horses

I smell the summer breeze with horse manure in the air
I stroll to the stable and then unlatch the door
My fingers tingle with excitement
I stroke the horse
He flaps his tail in excitement
And neighs
I get my brush out of the box and brush his silky skin
He taps his hoof on the floor.

I grab the halter rope and tack him up
His name is Glen
He swaggers along expecting a mint
I squelch through the mud to the field gate
I nearly fall over
I grab Glen and let him off into the field
He runs around like he's never seen today or tomorrow.

Albert Webb (14)
Caldecott Foundation School

Friends Poem

I am sitting down in my room crying on my window ledge
I am upset because I've found out that my best friend is gone
I know I will never see her again and I am scared of that
I don't know where she's gone.
Now I am lonely, on my own with no one to talk to but myself
There was me and you and I don't think I'll ever find someone
                                            as nice as you
I find myself going through all the films and photos we were in together
There's nothing to do now and I am bored
So what will I do when someone comes new?
I won't know what to say because . . . I am frightened of replacing you.

Theresa Tysoe (14)
Caldecott Foundation School

Music

I've got music in my room
I've got music on my iPod
I've got music in my soul
I play guitar like Paul Weller
I play guitar, it makes me feel good
When I feel the strings, they feel like bark
The guitar feels cold and hard, smooth, heavy
I strum the strings
I dream about being at the top one day
I get carried away playing my guitar
Tasha bangs on the door and tells me to stop
But I do not hear her so she comes in and tells me
To be quiet
I come back to reality
I'm just in my room
Playing my guitar.

Dwayne Thomas (13)
Caldecott Foundation School

Toast

I opened my eyes
Oh the smell wafting through the house
Toast
Wonderful, golden brown
Toast
At the beginning of every day . . .
Toast
Spread butter, jam and lots of sweet things . . .
Toast
Peanut butter, smooth and crunchy
Now that's the way I like my *toast.*

Ryan Brannigan (14)
Caldecott Foundation School

Feelings

Have you ever felt?
Well, have you?
I have and . . .
That's the truth
I have been feeling
Everything you have been dreaming of.

Can I tell you something I never felt?
Hand on my heart,
Truth from the start.

I have never felt
A feeling where it felt
Like I was dreaming.

I have never felt that feeling
Where all my dreams came true
I have never felt that feeling
As much as I love you.

Julianna Boateng (14)
Cator Park School for Girls

What Is Beauty?

Is beauty someone's face?
Is beauty your sense of taste?
Is beauty the way you speak?
Is beauty someone who's not a freak?
So what really is it all about?
Is it if you're loud
Or if you're proud?
I'm not quite sure
It could be even someone who's sick or poor
No one can quite see
Maybe it will come for free
Is beauty in me?

Sarah Burns (14)
Cator Park School for Girls

Troubled My Mind Is

I have too many worries on my mind
I have too many tears coming from my eyes
I feel so alone
In this huge world
I don't know what to do.

I sit by the bins outside my house
I hear loud noises from inside
I look to the window
And sit and stare
Why couldn't I be more like them?

I walk in the rain
With my head down
I don't know where I'm walking now
I hear a loud horn blaring in my ears
The next moment, I find myself on the floor, dead.

Why couldn't I have a happy life?
I was only 14
And look at me now.

Simara John (14)
Cator Park School for Girls

Death

Death is a beautiful thing,
Torture is deserved,
Payback comes in small doses.
Guns kill quick.
Knives need skill.
Poison can be drunk or sprinkled for the kill.
Murder can be hit and run on purpose
Gas used to smoke and steam
Fire used to burn and fry
Death.
Death.

Mica Walters (14)
Cator Park School for Girls

The Baby's Life Begins

I lie here staring into space
Waiting for a sound
The sound of voices, of footsteps coming down this way
I start to cry,
Hoping that the big, cuddly and caring giant comes to get me
The arms come slowly in my cot and pick me up
I stop crying
I find myself in a highchair with giants all around
And toys on the floor
I want to get out
I cry and cry
Hopefully someone will save me
But no, the giant comes in with a pot
And sits right in front of me
'Open wide,' the giant says
Yuck, I don't like porridge
I push away and cry
Finally someone lets me out
I'm free.

Kelly Walker (13)
Cator Park School for Girls

Waiting

I sit back, looking at the photos that cover my wall,
All of which now seem so long ago,
Faint memories now.
Remembering the day I watched you fade into the distance,
Driven away out of my reach, out of the station,
To go on your new journey.

Days together that we used to share,
Long nights up, talking,
Pulling up the pillows to keep imagining myself
Drifting off to sleep in the comfort of your arms once more.
Longing, waiting for you, anticipating your return . . .

Though my mind pictures
You being there, standing, waiting for me at the other end
To join you at your side.
When the time comes, that day arrives
I will be forever yours.

Jessica Nettell (16)
Cator Park School for Girls

Global Warming

Stop!
Just for one moment, drop
Everything you're doing!

Look around you, what can you see?
I see total devastation staring back at me.
We have to change our ways,
Or else we'll have to pay -
Let's do it!

For our generations yet to come
We have to be greener, everyone,
Walk, don't drive
To keep the world alive -
We can do it!

Please don't jump on planes
Whenever you see the rains,
Recycle, recycle every day
Recycle, recycle, that's the way -
We can do it!

We all must work together
To improve the weather,
It might be too late
Because we chose to wait -
I think we can do it!

Who am I kidding,
This world is bidding
Farewell to us all.
The icebergs are small -
I hope we can do it!

The problem gets bigger
But people just snigger,
Maybe we can't do it.

Charlotte Fuller (12)
Cator Park School for Girls

Death's Door

Good morning
Wake to the smell of hardcore drugs
Ready to sell another day
The phone's ringing
You know the deal
Already sold yourself

The fridge is empty
Yet your pocket is full
The hunger for more still grows
As you sit and wait
For your next customer
Already sold yourself

He arrives
Shirt buttoned low, barely dressed
Does it matter?
You package it up, no hesitation
Quick sniff before departure
Already sold yourself

Ring, ring, ring
Off you go
A lengthy journey worth every penny
You approach the steps of the door
One shot, two shot, three shot
Goodnight.

Hermione Salmon (16)
Cator Park School for Girls

Midnight Madness

For hundreds of years a story has been told
Of a witch so evil, bitter and old
The story of her made children weep
And parents on their children their eyes did keep
For many children went to play
In her forest not far away
But only a few of them did return
With such tales of horror and concern
Three naïve souls ventured there
Madness drove them to her lair
For they got lost on their way
Twisting in and out of the same trees, day by day
Such tragedies happened to them on their trip
Like agonising screams heard in the night and the crack of the whip
Soon three were to become two
As one of them was kidnapped, I wonder by who?
They searched for him everywhere
But nothing was found but the entrance to her lair
As the moon settled and night hung, they cowered away
But again, as before, they could hear screaming of such pain
This time they followed the trail of hurt
They should have run the opposite way as they had learnt
For they scrambled into her lair
And followed every creaky stair
Until they met their gloomy doom
Their innocent lives taken in that room
Their bodies have never been found
Though people say there is a horrid sound
Of screams and heckling during the hours of darkness
Made by the innocent souls of her midnight madness.

Millie Hayes (13)
Cator Park School for Girls

Peter Pan

I hang up the phone
A lump forms in my throat
My stomach knots itself
I feel as if I could float

I jump two stairs at a time
Crash into my room with glee
Switch on the radio
And pack my costume for Wendy

My shoes slap against the pavement
My bag bounces off my hip
I walk the alley humming
Through a door and backstage I slip

I am greeted by many faces
Some with face paint and mermaid tails
I smile and pull out my costume
A flowery nightdress with a pink that's pale

Hours come and hours pass
Scripts are flicked through then thrown aside
I wait nervously in the corridor
And go on stage with a smile that's wide

Hot lights shine on my grinning face
The play ends and I'm happy
I feel the buzz of being on stage
Then pack my things and climb into a taxi

I get home and sigh with relief
Notice the flashing of the answerphone light
I push the button and my jaw drops
Cos I have to do it again tomorrow night.

Laura Walton (13)
Cator Park School for Girls

Seeing Is Believing

There is darkness all around me
There is darkness closing in
I open my eyes wider now
Hoping that light will seep in.

I do not stumble in the darkness
For I know the many wheres
But when I fall into the darkness
No one comes, does no one care?

But wait - what's this?
A voice is coming that I know
A helping hand, a friendly word or two
They want to help, they tell me so.

And now there are people all around me
Voices growing fainter
I have to trust, I want to see
Will it work? I'll find out later . . .

And when I wake
I find I have to clamp my eyes tight shut
To stop the light from hurting
So very, very much.

But then the lights dim
And as they do, I open up my eyes
And I can *see!*
I can see at last, it's such a fantastic surprise.

They say seeing is believing
And that I truly believe!

Julia Margetts (11)
Cator Park School for Girls

My Magic Box

(Based on 'Magic Box' by Kit Wright)

In my magic box I would put . . .
My most treasured pictures
My first ever drawings
My first memory as a baby
My soft, cosy blanket
Roses and bluebells
And a chocolate-coloured puppy
My family and friends
The wonderful laughter of my niece.

In my golden sparkling box . . .
Would be my favourite DVD
My best clothes and shoes
Neatly placed in my box
Would sit a bottle of vanilla-scented perfume
With a massive box of Galaxy
My bouncy trampoline
My house and peaceful garden
My beloved teddies
Propped on top of my fluffy bed
For me to eat would be
A bag of juicy plums.

In my magic box would be . . .
My PG Tips
That I would drink
As I relax in the peacefulness of the sunset.

Louisa Burrows (12)
Cator Park School for Girls

Smile

Her smile set the sun to jealousy
And every night the moon would compete with her eyes
She had been everything
She had been his everything
She *had* been
The sun stopped shining as her feet left the bridge
The moon highlighted the blood that touched the river
That night, she had flown
That night, she had escaped.

The most beautiful smile can hide such a troubled mind
They called her dead, he called her angel
They called her ill, he called her free
The smile that hid a thousand words
The words that screamed inside her
Chose not to be heard.

Still she smiled that smile
The smile that plagues his mind
The bitter-sweet memory
No one deserves to remember
The smile she gave only to him
And he can take it no longer
He pulls the noose around his neck
And kicks the chair away . . .

And he flies.

Esme Tyler (13)
Cator Park School for Girls

Think Again

Shall I, shan't I?
Can I, can't I?
Will I, won't I?
Think again, I.

Want it; but
I know I shouldn't
Take it
No, I really couldn't.

Suit yourself
No, wait a minute
I haven't decided
I might just take it.

Shall you, shan't you?
Will you, won't you?
Can you, can't you?
Think again, you.

Really should take
Complete control
If you want to stay
Out of life's treacherous hole.

Rachel Tracey (15)
Cator Park School for Girls

Happy

What makes me happy?
A smile on a face
A summer's day
A day of fun
A laugh in the sun
A play with your friends
A dinner with your family
A memory that never ends
That's what makes me happy.

Lucy Shirley Paine (13)
Cleeve Park School

I Love Sport

I love all sports
cricket, football, all sorts.
Football is what I like most of all
I love to dribble and kick the ball.
All the time I'm up to play
anywhere, any day.
I also like to play cricket
I like to play keeper of the wicket.
I've got the stuff, like a bat
special pads and a special hat.
Tennis is a favourite of mine
scoring points most of the time.
Hitting the ball in the lovely sunshine
making it hit inside the baseline.
Basketball, my favourite sport
dribbling the ball up and down the court.
Left side, right side, down and up.
Scoring a goal to win a cup.
I love all sport as you can see
being a professional my life's fantasy.

Joe Drake (13)
Cleeve Park School

Happiness

Have you ever been so happy it makes you wild?
Have you ever been so happy it makes you laugh?
Have you ever been so happy that you went warm with a smile?
Have you ever been so happy that you feel like you rule?
Have you ever been so happy that you feel like the best?
Happiness with people makes you want to laugh
Give a cheesy grin and wave with a smile.

Harry Green (11)
Cleeve Park School

Kids In Jeopardy

Katy is a girl in her bed
Then she hears her dad coming up the stairs
She hides under the covers because she is so scared
But no one can hear her screams of terror in the bed.

Her dad blames her for all his faults
Even though Katy says sorry
Her dad punches her in the head
But now blood is pouring from her bed
Her dad walks away but he doesn't know she's dead.

Joshua Bowers (12)
Cleeve Park School

Love

Love is being alone with the one you love
Love is so romantic
Love brings smiles all around
Love is like the heat of the sun
Sometimes love can hurt
Love has to be true feelings
When he is around I am always happy.

Rebecca Cox (13)
Cleeve Park School

Happiness

Happiness is a peaceful day in the park
Happiness brings smiles all around
Happiness brings fun and joy
Happiness is always being there for your friends
When I'm around the ones I love I am so joyful
I jump up and down with joy.

Amy Dunn (12)
Cleeve Park School

Feelings

Depression is my name
I come about, no shame
Some names, I know a few
Every day I learn something new.

Confusion has walked through the door
All classes I don't know
Lots of faces around me
Hoping they'll be friendly.

Empty, there's nothing inside me
So let's keep this nice and simple
Having entered the classroom
So far only met one pupil.

Angry is my inner self
It's like I need some healing
If you push me too far
I might have to express my feelings.

Pius Inebode (12)
Cleeve Park School

Fear

Fear is . . .
Confused in the mind
Alone inside
Closed in around you
Terror stalks you
Coldness haunts you
Trapped without words
The world is black
Darkness hits you
Death freezes your movement . . .
Fear is the end of the world.

Rachel Brackpool (12)
Cleeve Park School

The Predator

I hate it, it wasn't me
Why did I get blamed?
I had to hit her
I just had to.

Sometimes I wish she could feel
As timid and insignificant as I
She is one of the school's important
She is a lion.

I wish she could feel fear
And as isolated as I
There she was waiting
For another prey.

A prey to trap and belittle
You will get it no matter what you do
You always will.

You can't rat or snitch on her
And sometimes I stand there thinking,
Why me?

Ib Onarinde (12)
Cleeve Park School

Fear

Fear every day at school
Scared of going around corners
To see if the bully is there
Sitting on my own at lunch
Feeling cold and sensitive
Left out because no one wants to play with me
And that's what my day is like
What it's like to be me at school every day.

Scott Best (12)
Cleeve Park School

The Boy At School

When I walk by he gives me butterflies
He makes me feel all shy inside
When he smiles I melt like butter
My heart skips a beat and then starts to flutter.

When I look into his eyes
So big, shiny and wise
I see the deep blue sea
But sadly, he isn't looking back at me.

I can't wait each day to go back to school
To see the boy that makes me drool!

Jamilia Sooh (11)
Cleeve Park School

Untitled

Standing on the street, I've been rejected
My friends have gone, I'm lost
I feel hated and bullied, will I survive?
Sweat drips from my head as tears drop from my eyes
I'm scared.

The phone slips from my hand as I go to reach it
The sky is getting darker by the minute
Nobody's here, I'm alone
Abandoned by the world, what to do?
I don't know.

Scott Merkell (12)
Cleeve Park School

Fear

Fear is a hurtful emotion
Fear is when you are petrified of something you don't like
Fear is when you cry and you feel like breaking down
Fear is like a phobia, when you are scared of heights, spiders
and flying
Fear is when you feel sad and insecure
Fear is when you are rejected by other people and they leave you out
Fear can be depression if you feel worried
We all fear all these things
We wish we didn't have to fear everything in the world
But some people will always fear all these things.

Darius Groeger (13)
Cleeve Park School

Happiness To Me

H igh spirits
A musements on a happy day
P erseverance in something which makes you happy
P eople around you
I dyllic day full of happiness
N ot loneliness but happiness
E quality with your family
S miling on a happy day
S pecial day
Happiness to me is . . .

Michelle Zviripayi (13)
Cleeve Park School

France

When we went to France
It was very hot
The car was red-hot
The sun was white-hot
It was lovely.

When I saw the dolphins in the aquarium
Marvelling at their majestic beauty
Their strength and speed
The show was great
It was like watching a deer dashing and darting in the forest.

The lovely golden beaches.
The sea was lovely and warm
Swimming in the sea was lovely
The sea lapping against me
The warm breeze blowing against me.

The food was lovely
Proper French chips and steak
I wouldn't go near the frogs and snails though
The freshly cooked food
The juicy steak was lovely
I'm so happy.

Matthew Higgs (11)
Cleeve Park School

Happiness

I feel so happy inside I just found out my surprise
My friends are starting to arrive, I can't believe my surprise
Receiving my presents from all of my friends
My surprise is driving me round the bend
I feel so warm inside
Finally I'm starting to unravel my surprise
Can you guess it?
I'm going to the . . . *seaside!*

Danni Rouse (11)
Cleeve Park School

Thank You

Thank you for my food
I enjoy every meal
Thank you for my medicine
That takes away the pain and heals.

Thank you for books
That I learn and read from
Thank you for the earth
That I plant and grow a seed from.

Thank you for my learning
That leads to a career
Thank you for all the celebrations
In each and every year.

Thank you for the water
That helps me in many ways
Thank you for the clothes I wear
Al the nights and days.

But some kids don't have food
They starve on the streets
And even if they're super good
They can't have any treats.

Some kids can't celebrate
'Cause there isn't a reason to
When they are poor
And don't know what to do.

Thank you for all of these things
That lighten up my way
And help me to remember all the poor people
Living on the streets today.

Louise Smith
Cleeve Park School

Sadness

This is how I feel;
Cold, weak, upset, lonely, bitter, empty
I look around the playground
No one comes to me
My clothes keep them away
A very long way away
I am imprisoned in myself
Because I will always be sad.

Shyan Sittampalam (12)
Cleeve Park School

The Maze Of Romance

Romance is like a maze
Long and confusing
Go the right way and you're fine
Go the wrong way and your life
Will fall apart before your very eyes
Send your soul into the realm of depression
Hate, anger and emptiness . . .
This is the road I took.

Phillip White (13)
Cleeve Park School

The Snow Day

The best part of being happy is playing in the snow
The expressions on the children's faces is such a warming glow
Their cheesy grins make you smile
As they dive into a giant snow pile.

James Rogers (11)
Cleeve Park School

No One Can Escape Fear

Fear is being scared of your own shadow
Fear is shaking under your bedsheet
Fear is being frightened of everything that moves
Fear is shivering cold in the dark, scary night
Fear is being disliked and rejected by other people
Fear is being down and depressed
Fear is being upset and crying with no company but your own
These are the things people feel every day all over the world
The weird thing is, no one can escape it.

James Arsmtrong (13)
Cleeve Park School

Bad Loser

Anger is about being trapped,
Humpy, frustrated and red
Overall when I lose
I just can't help myself
Like a tornado I go
Ripping through the room
I can't help myself
I'm just a bad loser.

Shaun Brown (11)
Cleeve Park School

Anger

All on my own, my face is so red
I have not a clue why I have been sent to bed
I feel so stressed, I thought I was the best
But now I know I am really a pest.

Tobie Mitchell (13)
Cleeve Park School

Ireland

When I knew we were going to Ireland
I was . . . over the moon
That I would be seeing Jamie soon
The Kildare breeze
As I walk in the town
It makes me feel warm and loved
As I see green fields
With sheep running free
I sit inside with a warm cup of tea
Rabbits on the hills
As the night draws in
That's the happiness Ireland brings.

Amy O'Connor (11)
Cleeve Park School

What Is It?

I'm alone in the world
I'm here alone
Hey, what's that over there?
Look, look, it's only got one hair
I stand up slowly and reach for the light
It makes a noise and gives me a fright
The light is here, get ready to jump
It falls off the chair with a bump
The light is on, oh look, it's Dad
I must, I must be going mad.

Faye Donohoe (11)
Cleeve Park School

Fear

It was in the dead of night
When I had a fright
I got out of bed
When someone said,
'Go back, go back, go back to sleep.'
That's when I knew I had to creep
I was cold and alone
When off went the phone
So I picked it up and put it to my ear
But there was no one to hear
I put the phone aside
I was terrified
There was a sound
And as I turned around
I made a frown
Because out of the darkness
Came a smiling clown!

Tom Moore (11)
Cleeve Park School

Depression/Happiness

Depression
Is when you are sad
Insecure, left out
Angry with yourself
This is what I feel like sometimes.

Happiness
Is when you are enjoying life
Fun, sunny days
Being with your family
This is how I feel sometimes.

Cameron Terry (13)
Cleeve Park School

Louder Than Nothing

All cold and alone
I sit upon the highest tower
Watching, waiting
I see her; the single soul in a swarm of millions
Who needs me the most
She comes, she stays, she sits beside me
But never sees me, never hears me
Always has known me
We sit, I listen, I do what I do best
She screams, she cries, calls out a plea
I hug her, hold her
But she is never aware that I am here
Slowly she stops, gives herself to me
I finally wrap my arms around her like a soft blanket
And she sleeps.

When she wakes I am still here holding her tightly
Every word she tells herself
Every sound she makes burns a hole into my soul
I cover her, try to stop her but it is too late
She tries to scream, I cover her
She tries to cry, I cover her
Her tears are shed, I cover her
She cannot take it,
She runs back to the one place
I can only go to after life
I sit again on top of my tower
And my echo is silence
And my echo is silence
And my echo is so silent everyone hears me
I am louder than life
Yet no one hears me
I am louder than everything
Yet nothing hears me
My true form has no shape
My true life has no death
In the echo of nothing
I live.

Scarlett Chapman (14)
Combe Bank School

Trapped In Here

I sit here lonely,
Lonely I am,
Sitting here,
Like a lost lamb.

My heart is filled,
With anger and rage,
As I sit here still,
In this cage.

I remember those days,
When I was a cub,
I used to laugh and play,
And eat all my grub.

The king of the jungle,
The king of the beasts,
But not anymore,
Unless released.

My family in Africa,
Having such fun,
Until they hear,
The shooting of the gun.

Staring outside,
I see humans roam,
I wish I was free,
Back at home.

My wild instincts,
Now all gone,
A life as a lion,
Sad and forlorn.

My future in this world is bleak,
But I will never admit defeat.

Yuk Yee Vuong (12)
Dartford Grammar School for Girls

Life

Life is like a step
Choose which step to take
If you take the wrong one
You will make a mistake.

Life is like a roller coaster
Going up and down
Facing light and darkness
Dreaming through the dawn.

Life is like a dream
A dream to fulfil
Life is a hope
A hope not to kill.

When you are in trouble
There is always a hand
God will always help you
When you are to land.

Life is a beauty
Through beauty I glow
Life is a pain
Through pain I grow.

Trust in Jesus
In Jesus I trust
Call and He will answer
Help you - He will just.

Life is love
Love that comes from a divine creation
Feel this with compassion
This is the spiritual revelation.

Infanta Suganthanaikabahu (12)
Dartford Grammar School for Girls

To Be A Baby

To be a baby
It helps if you're able
To give the biggest smile
To hypnotise the public
And can give the biggest
Squishiest hug to get the
Attention from everyone else.

To be a baby
It helps to have
A big bright dummy to dip in jam
And a two-handled bottle
With warm milk inside
It helps to have
A warm fluffy blanket
To set the 'cute' image.

These are the stock-in-trade
The public demands
Without which no claim
To be a baby
Can be considered serious.

But truly to be a baby
What you need is
The strongest of lungs
So you can be heard
Wherever you are
You need the energy to
Wake everyone all through the night.

Olivia Searle (13)
Dartford Grammar School for Girls

Where Will We Be?

Where will I be? Where will you be?
When our dead young dreams have whispered away
Scattered by the wind.
How will I know that I will always feel
Your silver kiss imprinted, always you.

How will I know? How will you know?
That I echo Earth's lust-long sigh of memory
Trailing your name without me
How will I know that you will remember us . . .
Forgotten? Obscure reverie.

How can I be sure that you are sure?
That our stars will cross for a second time
Under endless rafters of sky
But do you not know that clouds obscure the sun
Dark complexion of destiny.

How can you look at me and me back at you
When we both know we're a lie.
Two bleeding empty wounds
Now you can see me through your burning eyes
My winter tears, vacant fears.

How do I leave? How do you leave?
When our souls are so entwined
And the deep is so wish-cold
How do I swim now or keep my head afloat
Amidst the white masks of my tears?

How do I stop it hurting when you are gone?
And I smell your incense burn and there is pain
How do I choke my mouth when I miss you too much?
In my midnight trance, screaming silence. Call for you.

Where will my hopes go? Where will your dreams reside?
Outside our lives now, blank canvas energy
Will someone else paint upon my dreams with you?
Dancing over them, devoid of me.

Will I be able to hear you laugh or will you sense me smile?
When the seasons change and time's fine grains begin to slip
Will my feelings always mean so much or will they turn water red?
Expired love, dismissed as lust.

Can you not hear that I'm crying now
Loss of pretty words you'll never hear
I'll miss you like . . .
Like I've never missed
Illusion strange to me
Lost and gone
Lonely.

Rachel Long (18)
Dartford Grammar School for Girls

Anorexic

As fat as a hippo, chubby and round,
I can't stand to look; I look to the ground.
Obviously the mirror lies,
It must see the pain in my eyes,
The reflection I see,
It's not what I want to be.
I'm so hungry, I haven't eaten for days,
I keep getting told that I'm wasting away,
As thin as a pin; as skinny as a rake,
I feel my body start to shake,
But I carry on through the pain,
My body's slowing down again,
But the rolls and the folds are all still there,
It's just too disgusting to bear.
It's almost like people want me to be fat
And they think I should accept it, just like that.
Well, I won't, it's too bad
You're driving me mad.

Abbie Noakes (13)
Dartford Grammar School for Girls

To Be A Bathroom Cupboard

To be a bathroom cupboard
It helps if you're able
To take the pressure
Of all the bath presents your owners got
But never used
Like all the bath fizzers
Shower gel too
And when guests come to stay
You have to keep locked away
All the disgusting things they do!

To be a bathroom cupboard
It helps to have
A mirror attached
To watch your owner
Pluck, squeeze and wax
And you must have shelves inside
To hold up all the tacky things
And not forgetting a handle
To fit their hand into yours!

But to truly be a bathroom cupboard
What you need is
To be stored in a bathroom
And to store packets inside
That hold ranges of things
That will rarely be used
But when your owner sings
You keep it inside your door
And don't tell a soul
You have to keep secrets
Of course you will, so no one will ever know!

Charlotte Sloan (12)
Dartford Grammar School for Girls

Wild Horses

The undisturbed snow lay glistening, peaceful, calm and fresh
Waiting for the imprints of hooves to be displayed on its soft surface
Waiting, waiting, waiting . . .
The explosion of the thunderous beat of hooves
Came galloping down the snowy hills.

Storming colours of darkest brown, dapple-grey and mysterious black
Spreading across the hills
The determination of the horses was to be desired
The ice-spray of a sea in their wake
A sprinkle of icing on the dark fairy cakes
Sparkling, sparkling, sparkling . . .

A thousand diamonds filled the sky
As power and strength came galloping by
Like engines constantly changing hue
Free to fly with wings unseen
Soaring, soaring, soaring . . .
Like a river bursting through a dam
Surging, roaring, forever onwards and peace.

Lydia Caplan (13)
Dartford Grammar School for Girls

Away With Words

A picture tells a thousand words,
A glance can tell a tale,
A gesture can do wonders
When speech has seemed to fail.
An action can be fatal.
It can pierce the heart and mind,
But if it is used properly
You may begin to find
That it can be a blessing,
It can make somebody's day
So don't fret when words have vanished,
You don't need them anyway.

Jody Bloom (14)
Dartford Grammar School for Girls

Life

Maybe dreams cannot come true
But maybe you just have to believe in you
Points to guide us are on the way
Don't give up or be a stray
If we never get that far
There's always your family, your guiding star.

Never let anyone get to you
Your friends are here and others too
Having had the courage to say no
Live your life fully, you must go
Take the chances you are offered
Even if you're not that bothered.

Happiness is not easily found
Keep your eyes up from the ground
To the heavens and the skies above,
The most important thing is love,
Living your days happily,
This is life, you will see.

Emily Howkins (13)
Dover College

There Once Was A Rabbit

(In memory of my grandad)

There once was a rabbit
Developed the habit
Of twitching the end of his nose
His sisters and brothers
And various others, said,
'Notice the way that it goes.'

Now, one clever bunny said,
'That's very funny
I'll practise it down in the dell.'
And he did and she did
And they did and we did
And did it remarkably well.

So now the world over
Where bunnies eat clover
And burrow and scratch with their toes
There isn't a rabbit who hasn't the habit
Of twitching the end of his nose.

Sam Hubbard (13)
Dover College

The Meaning Of Life

Are you here for your sake or others?
When people are teasing will they listen?
Are they to *be* inspired or *to* inspire?
Does it mean more to inspire
People older than you?
If you chose, you could live more in a week
Than some people do in a lifetime.

All you need to do is go.

You should think there is happiness
In the darkest of times
It is not the end
But the beginning.
Will you be honest
In the face of others?
If you can think about your life ahead
You can change it.

Tom Robson (13)
Dover College

Being A Winner

Who can climb the highest mountain of all?
You can
Who can complete the hardest race of all?
You can
Who can sail around the globe in record time?
You can
Never give up on your dreams
No matter how hard or tough it gets
But don't make dreams your master
You can do anything you want in the world
If you really want it and you commit yourself to it
You will achieve, I have no doubt of that
The world is yours
And what is more, you will be a winner, my friend.

Josh Corney (13)
Dover College

Never-Ending Lover

My love, I have tried with all my being
To grasp a comparable to thine own
But nothing seems worthy.

I know now why Shakespeare could not
Compare his love to a summer's day
It would be a crime to denounce the beauty
Of such a creature as thee
To simply cast away the precision
God has placed in forging you.

Each facet of your being
Whether it physical or spiritual
Is an ensnarement
From which there is no release
I wish to stay entrapped forever
With you for all eternity
Our hearts, always as one.

Peter Vickerman (14)
Dover College

Life

If you have a dream
You have to have a scheme
Work to the limits and achieve
Your goal.
Every minute is crucial
You have to be official
But always be initial
But not unofficial.

Don't give up on life
Or life gives up on you
But think of the rewards in life
And always achieve your goal.

Chandy Castle (14)
Dover College

14

Life is life
You know it all
You could be tall
You could be small
You could be lazy
You could be fat
But when you're my age - that is that!

Life is difficult
Life is easy
When I'm alone
It's all breezy
But when I'm at school
I act the fool
Want to break out
Want to look cool.

Now I realise I've got to grow up
And not care how I'm seen
Got to grow up, got to grow up
Now that I'm 14.

Richard Bowen (14)
Dover College

The Meaning Of Life

The meaning of life is to succeed
But first you must sweat and bleed
And try your best, don't be a sheep
And follow the rest
You may like maths
You may like sports
It's your choice
Whatever it is, do your best
To do it and don't listen
To those who tease
They are full of spite
Just do your best, that's my dream!

Jack Hennessey (13)
Dover College

The Meaning Of Life

What is the meaning of life?
Is it all tears, woe and strife
Or is it just being a woman and being a wife?

You never know what you're doing next
Maybe calling someone or writing a text
Knowing someone is there for you
Makes you want to be there for them too.

Girly things
Fluttering wings
Little things
Tickling things.

School is a way of learning
Although you know that things may be turning.

Make-up here
Make-up there
Make-up everywhere
On your floor
On your bed
On your dressing table
Or maybe in your shed?

A girl's life . . .
But what else does it mean?

Amy Rollinson (14)
Dover College

Friends

I like insects
I like carrots
I like jelly
I like chocolate
My favourite colour is pink
My favourite TV programme is 'Friends'
My best friend is Kyile
Kyile likes carrots
Kyile doesn't like loud noise
Sometimes Kyile feels cross
Sometimes Kyile pinches my jumper
That makes me sad
But when Kyile says sorry
We can be friends again.

Kyile White & Louise Godin (15)
Glyne Gap School

Oh-4-Oh-2-Oh-7

Existence again . . .
The point is lost
A life for nothing
Not worthy the cost
Of what we go through
To get to the end
Of all things real
None will kneel
A cracked wall
A fractured pride
Always in this world
And always denied
The pleasure of being
Allowed to be free
From the shackles of life
And its tyranny.

Sam Mattacott (15)
Gravesend Grammar School for Boys

Battle Of The Sky

Yellow streak, secretly snaking, slicing across the sky,
The gold glimmer of hope visible for a saffron second,
Before, in a flash, once again the dark raven cape reigns.

A loud warcry echoes deep from the heavens above,
Tiny glass daggers rapidly spearhead through the air,
Shattering noisily against the floor one after another,
Each droplet piercing the sky, ever falling, ever faster.

Lightning sharp as a sword rapidly cracks the sky,
Breaking the defence, the barrier before being withdrawn,
Another attempt to crush the ebony evil fails.

As another angry roar emerges, screaming of destruction,
Of God's wrath, an apocalypse, the end of humanity.

Gold now flashes frequently, dancing elegantly, weaving intricately,
The cloud wanes, allows a bright silver moon to appear,
Destroying the large black mass, freeing the sky, forcing victory.

Robert Humphries (14)
Gravesend Grammar School for Boys

Rainbow

R ed, orange, yellow, green, blue, indigo and violet
A rching across the sky
I s there really a pot of gold at the end?
N otice how the colours merge
B eaming across the sky
O ur eyes delight in its presence
W ondering how long it will last.

Matthew Blakemore (15)
Gravesend Grammar School for Boys

Adjusting

You can bury your head,
You can stand still and wait,
Remember what it was they said -
'It's never too late'.
Eyes begin to widen to it
It's not what it used to be
There's no point in a sit,
Got to get up and see;
That realising the new,
It won't tarnish the old
That's what you got to do
Can't linger on stories told.
Can't always be rainbows and light
The dark just has to come too,
Because that's the contrast, right?
Yeah, that's what you got to do.
That age when you see it clear
It hits you fast, hits you hard
Just keep those friends near,
And try to pull down that façade;
It helps.

Nicholas Wilson (14)
Gravesend Grammar School for Boys

What Are We?

What are we doing here?
In society, what is our job?
Is it to insult, heckle and jeer?
We are here, classed as 'yob'.
Do we provide any use to our neighbourhood?
They say all we do is murder and stab.
In the eyes of society, we never do any good.
All we ever do is steal and nab.
'Hoodies', 'yobs' and 'vandals',
That's all we hear every single day.
We never go to church lighting candles,
We'd rather light up a fag they say.
We deal in drugs all the time,
We've got our own language, too.
None of us are fazed by crime
But I'll tell you something and it's true
Look out world
We are the future.

Darren Horner (14)
Gravesend Grammar School for Boys

The Smog

Silence . . .
The air is thick with fog
The air has a certain absence
It's back, I can see it, the *smog*.

Now I can hear people running and screaming
The sirens bellowing out endless streams of sound
The air is thick and seething
The endless images of smoke going around and around.

Something strikes me in the back of the head
I'm not sure how long I can last
I touch the back of my skull, I bring it back and can see it's blood-red
I didn't hear the bang behind me, the blast.

Time slips by and I notice nothing
I'm finding it hard to go on
The clock in my head has stopped ticking
Lying on the hard rock which I have fallen upon.

I feel that I can come to no harm
And as I lie here and slog
I feel something brush past my arm
Oh no, it's back, the *smog!*

Tom Harper (15)
Gravesend Grammar School for Boys

Love Will Be Your Demise - Haiku

A woman or girl
Can fill your heart forever
Or rip it to shreds!

Danny Payne (14)
Gravesend Grammar School for Boys

A Midwinter's Day Cheating

Tottenham's fans stop to cheer
Man U's fans start to sneer
Ronaldo took a dive to the floor
And Spurs had lost hope for evermore.

Spurs play incredibly well
Man U deserve to rot in Hell
When Spurs are just about to rise
Man U led them to their demise.

Ronaldo scores Man U's stunning first
Spurs bow their heads and begin to curse
Malbranque and Ronaldo don't ever touch
Was the referee bribed? If so, just how much?

One, two, three and four goals,
I can't fill in the holes
Ronaldo just doesn't seem to stop cheating
Is that the reason Spurs took such a beating?

Ricky Dhami (14)
Gravesend Grammar School for Boys

If I Fail

If in my quest to achieve my goals
If I stumble, fall and lose my soul
If those that knew me would easily consign
Then there was never a life as hard as mine
No hope, no chance and no guide
I only follow my voice inside
If it guides me wrong and I do not win
Then I'll learn from my mistakes and try to achieve again.

Connor O'Flynn (14)
Gravesend Grammar School for Boys

Global Warming

This land once flourished
Plants bloomed in the field
Crops sufficiently nourished
What times of rich yield

We dined well those years
Countless crops to choose from
Never one of our fears
That all joy would be gone

The children are fading
Rain no longer falls
Our town ceases trading
Food production stalls

Our crops are failing
The sun gets intense
The babies are wailing
This all makes no sense

This land once flourished
But nothing blooms in the field
Crops insufficiently nourished
No more rich yield

Too much sun
Where is all the rain?
This is no longer fun
Slowly we die in pain.

James Simmons (15)
Gravesend Grammar School for Boys

Issues

The birds are tweeting in the trees,
The fish are swimming in the seas,
The cars are zooming past nearby
And the planes are flying in the sky.

Oil is drilled from the ocean bed,
All the birds in the barn are fed,
Coal is dug up from the ground
And in the local a lonely drink is downed.

Mobile buzzing on the train,
Car accident, people in pain,
Children buying sweets at the nearest shop
And youths talking to the local cop.

Birds stop tweeting in the chopped-down trees,
Fish caught and eaten from their seas,
Traffic clogging the road nearby
And the planes are polluting our beautiful sky.

Oil run out in the ocean bed,
Flu in the barn where the birds were fed,
Very little coal left in the ground
And in the pub an alcoholic's drink is downed.

Annoying mobile music filling the train,
Speed driving causes accidents and pain,
Fat kids stuffing faces in the shop
And youths questioned on robbery by the cop.

Jonathan Beresford (15)
Gravesend Grammar School for Boys

Dreams Come True

This is the one
This is my day
Where I will be transported
Far, far away.

To my land of dreams
I will head
To my land of paradise
Where special words will be said.

To unite me and her
For the rest of our lives
With no dips and swoops
And certainly no dives.

Our love will be lingering
Like a sweet perfume
No bad turns, for our love
To turn to doom.

I feel no negatives
I feel no doubt
My life will be turned
Inside out.

No more complications
No more insecurities
I feel nothing at all
To keep me from doing this day.

My dream is coming true
It's fair to say
This is the one
This is my day.

Robb Henderson (15)
Gravesend Grammar School for Boys

Reconciliation Is Misrepresentation

Light to dark, night to day,
Searching for the unknown,
Always looking with eyes closed,
Although I'll find you,
You can never be found.

There once was something in your eyes,
But all that's left is shame and disgrace.
Seeing isn't always being,
Although being is seeing beyond.
The lies behind the truth.

Wisdom is nothing,
Fools' fortune is everything.
The fools lead the wise,
Blind to their own ability.
Wisdom is not wise.

The words are there,
But they will never be heard.
The locked-away secret,
Taken to the grave.
These lips are always open.

Trust in deception,
A man is an island,
Floating alone, free to be,
An island has no purpose
It is free to be its own.

Thomas Saunders (15)
Gravesend Grammar School for Boys

A Life In Black And White

I once knew colour
Far from a world that only knows black and white
I was looking for a life less duller
And stumbled upon paradise
When Heaven and sky entwine
Beyond the furthest reaching eye
Such colour you could not refine
Awaited me that fateful night
A colour for every emotion
Every feeling
Every notion
My own personal coloured ocean.

Red would get my heart rate soaring
And ignite an emotional outpouring
Orange would make me feel vibrant and young
Making me forget all the times I'd been stung
Yellow gave me higher minded ideas
It gave me no time to remember my fears
Balance was the quality of green
It created in my mind a tranquil scene
The colour blue gave me inspiration
Released me from my constant frustration
And purple reignited my spiritual side
Which had once before long ago died.

But then I remembered
This was not right
And then life returned
To being black and white.

Brendan Johnson (14)
Gravesend Grammar School for Boys

Foxhunt

I sprint, heart pounding in my chest,
My paws beating a harsh rhythm
Across the rolling field, my home,
My failure will make it my grave.

I hear a bark, my head jerks round,
A flash of brown cresting the hill.
I cannot go any faster
And still they are gaining!

At last refuge!
I spring inside the hollow husk,
I greedily gulp down the air,
They hunt outside, they bark,
A death knell beating out its pitiless tune.

Moments pass like hours,
Have they gone? Can I be free?
Silent as the tread of time I creep,
To the end of my salvation and my prison.

A quick glance around,
Turning my ears, straining for
The telltale stray bark,
Where are they . . . ?

A growl from above,
My number's up, my time has come,
The vicious teeth spring towards me,
A moment of agony and then it ends
I end.

Jonathan Foster (15)
Gravesend Grammar School for Boys

Going To Hell Poem

I was gloomily wandering the streets that night
People were strange and merciless in this dim fog
As if they knew the thing that I was about to do
Urging me on, pushing me through, I don't know what I should do.

But they don't matter to me, I don't care what they think
They are just others, they don't know me inside
Why did they hate me? What had I done?
I couldn't ignore them, though I tried to hide
They're like everyone else and when I tried to befriend them
they'd just chide.

The people at school and even at home called me names every day
Some of them are 'Goth', 'Grunger', 'Satanist', even 'Gay'
Their words hit me like poisoned daggers,
I was fed up, I couldn't take it anymore
I was hurting, my heart was sore, I'd walk down this street where
I wanted to go
Through all the hurt I couldn't even walk, I was so determined,
I'd just staggered.

I was there, I was where I thought I wanted to be
This would be where my life would end
It would all be over, the end's where the pier juts out
I was going to run and then I'd drop, I'd hit the water and then I'd stop
My plunge halted as I breathed in the muddy water, my mind fought,
but in it gave
My consciousness was going, all was black, it was like
the deepest cave.

I thought I wouldn't do it, I thought I'd chicken out
But that is what *they'd* want and that's what this was about
I fell and fell, I thought I'd fall forever
There was suddenly light and burning heat
And before I knew it I was in *Hell!*

I never bullied and I never stole
So what's with the fire, what's with the coal?
Why am I here, what did I do? You bullied me, not I you
I'm in Hell, do you feel happy you put me here?
I'm gonna be here forever with all of my fears!

Sean Walsh (14)
Gravesend Grammar School for Boys

I'm Not OK

There is no need for a proper introduction
Let's get straight to the point
I'd look in the mirror and not like what I'd see
But what did you expect?
I'm not OK.

All those steps I'll never take
All those hearts I'll never break
All those things I'll never see
So many things I'll never be
Because I'm not OK.

The lights were low, my hands were shaking
The lights were dim, my heart was racing
Then it happened
It was my time
I was not OK.

Try to get my teen heart beating
I'll be holding on
I hope to God it was worth it
Because your love is the most deserving of
The worst thing I can say,
'So long and goodnight.'
I'm not OK.

Every day you wish you're someone you're not
How do you feel? That is the question
You'll find out firsthand what it's like to be me
I'm not OK.

When you're sitting alone inside your head
There'll be one thing left to say,
'You're not OK.'

Kyle Ludlow (15)
Gravesend Grammar School for Boys

I

I get temperamental at times,
I have the right.
I get under my parents' skin,
I have the right.
I am told I am idle at times,
I have the right.
I think I know what I want out of life,
I have the right.
I get bad acne,
I have the right.
I hate being wrong,
I have the right.
I am not the same as the rest,
I have the right.
I am a menace to society,
I have the right.
I am a teenager!

Manbir Mand (15)
Gravesend Grammar School for Boys

Sad Sally

Someone bought me for Lee
But he does not feed me
They hit me
My legs hurt as well
I'm only a dog
But they don't care about me
I cry and whimper
If I bark they say 'Go to your bed'.
If I don't go to bed
They will hit me so hard
If they do not stop hitting me
They will kill me
I hate these people.

Victoria Ross (15)
Harbour School

Homelessness

A nd they hit me
N o one believes me
G o away and leave me alone
E yes are staring at my ragged clothes
R unning from Hell.

S taring at me
H orrible to me
E yes are staring at me
L onely, all by myself
T easing me
E verybody doesn't believe me
R ude to me.

Caroline Piercey (14)
Harbour School

Grumpy Teenager

I think I am cool
I am dressed in black
My music's loud
I play great pool.

I fight with my brother
I think that's fair
I eat junk food
I am a cool dude.

They see a spoilt brat
They think I'm a prat
I play rap music
I wear hoodies.

Rhys Mitchell (15)
Harbour School

Anger

A nd they don't see me
N o luck seems to hit me
G oing somewhere else to live
E yes ignore me
R ushing in front of me

L ove me they don't
O nly talking to people they know
N o one stops and nods at me
L eaving me alone
E mpty the streets shall be
Y elling in the dark

T elling me to clear off
E yes on me every time
R unning over my bed
R ude to me
I nvisible they think
F riendly they are not
I ll they will make me
E mpty my stomach shall be
D estroying my things.

Paul Leatham (14)
Harbour School

Terrible Teenager

They think I'm a thug, is it the clothes I wear?
Tattoos and box hats do not make me a thug.
Inside I'm me, see beyond that first meet
I don't swear or punch the people I greet.

Josie Mockett (15)
Harbour School

Lost And Lonely Child

A nd they smacked me hard
'N ow go to bed,' they said
G et up the stairs
E yes need to be shut
R ude little girl

L et me out of my room, please
O h no
S orry for being naughty
T ough, you are not coming down

A nd annoying
L eave me alone
O h no, please, you're hurting me
N ever stop fighting them off
E ars hear silence.

Gemma Chapman (14)
Harbour School

Troubled Teenager

H ow can anyone think of me as a threat?
O ther people look away
O r avoid eye contact
D esperate to be seen
I wish to be heard
E ven looked at
S ome people don't do that ever

R ebels in the making
E nding up being left out
S uperior to everyone
P eople hanging out
E ventually people see
C oolness rules
T oday is our day.

Ivan Hunter-Johnson (15)
Harbour School

Lost Cat

A bandoned I am, I'm just a cat
N o one feeds me, love me I beg
G ive me a home, I'm yours to have
E verything I had now is gone
R emember me, I'm lost and scared

A bandoned I am, I'm just a cat
N o one loves me, take me back
G ive me food and love I beg
E veryone hates me, take me please
R emember me please, please, please

A nyone there for me to love?
N o one cares that I'm here
G ive me a home, please I beg
E verything I had now is gone
R emember me, I'm scared and alone.

Sasha Smith (15)
Harbour School

Dog Who Looked Like A Log

There was a dog
That was as fat as a log
He always galloped to its food
Then ate it like a slob, he was very rude
As he slept he looked like a cat
They tripped over him as he was fat
If you had fudge
He would give you a nudge
Vets said he should eat no more
Otherwise he wouldn't fit through the door
He dropped down dead
Everyone said he was overfed.

Kacie Hawkins (12)
Herne Bay High School

Why Is The Sea Salty?

There was a beautiful cave full of crystals
Precious crystals that shone in the daylight
The cave lay in the middle of the sea
No one would dare go in there
It was believed that there was a furious monster guarding the crystals.

There was a greedy man who wanted all the crystals for himself
So he sailed and sailed across the sea to get the precious crystals
He found no monster, but very heavy crystals.

He put all the very heavy crystals on his boat
But once he got on the boat, it instantly sank.

The man unfortunately drowned
But the most important thing
Is that the crystals melted in the sea
And turned the sea salty
That's why the sea is salty.

Lauren Hopkins (11)
Herne Bay High School

Sleepy Beauty

I've been asleep for ages
And I'm bored
Phone that Princy bloke
And tell him to hurry up
Can I have some food?
Ice cream, cake, burgers, chips, yum
When I get out I'm going to have a proper party
I need a bath
I need a new dress
I need my MP3 iPod, my CD player, my new phone
It's probably old now
Oh my God, hurry up Prince!

Jasmine Thomas (11)
Herne Bay High School

The Volcano

It bubbles under the surface of the molten rock
Hot magma is slowly turning to lava
Squeezing through the chamber
And then suddenly shooting up the volcano
The volcano is very violent by now
It shocks everything around
Everything tries to escape
But it's too late for anything
As it's going to explode
Any
Minute
Now
Kaboom!

The volcano is slowly weakening
Everyone sighs in relief because it's over
The scenery is blackened with soot and ash
The trees are dead and have suffered
It's the end of life around the volcano
Except the volcano who is laughing
The lava is rapidly running into molten rock
The eyes of the volcano slowly shut
It's dormant now, just sleeping
But you don't know when it will erupt next . . .

Fred Pearce (13)
Herne Bay High School

Robbers

The robbers on the run
I hate those worthless scum
Oh if I found a gun
I'd shoot them in the lung.

Joshua Walton (13)
Herne Bay High School

Just A Child

She screams, she screams
But no one hears
She cries, she cries
The cries of fear
She wonders, *what if, what if*
Or *when will I be free?*
Free to fly, free to see
Her dreams have all gone
But her hopes still live on!

She wonders, she wonders
All through the night
The fear still remains
I wonder what he's going to do tonight?
I feel so afraid, I feel so alone
I told my mum but she believes him over me
How could she do this, do this to me?
Now I guess I will never be *free!*

Sadie Williams (14)
Herne Bay High School

It Doesn't Matter

Everyone is a human being
So keep on living, seeing and believing
It doesn't matter if you're black or white
So take off your boots and stop this fight
It doesn't matter where you're from
We should all just get along.

It doesn't matter if you're tall
It doesn't matter if you're small
It doesn't matter if you're big
It doesn't matter if you're thin
We are all human in different ways.

Jamie Robertson (12)
Herne Bay High School

Love - I Wish

He told me he loved me
I guess I was wrong
I thought I was his everything
Turns out I was his nothing
I thought I'd found my prince
Turns out he already had a Cinderella.

I wish, I wish
I wish he still loved me
I wish, I wish
I wish he still cared
I wish, I wish
I wish I was his Cinderella.

I will always love him
I will always care
I will always be there
To hold him and care.

I just wish he would love me
I wish he would care
I wish he would be there
To hold me and care . . .

I wish he loved me.

Naomi Hougham (14)
Herne Bay High School

Playing The Game

Up an down the court we run
The ball seems to be like a sun
Everyone is fighting for the ball
We aren't getting a goal at all.

We are losing now, 16-1
I think this match should be done
Here we are, one week later
I think QE will be a hater.

The game has started
And the team has parted
3-0, the QEs are ahead
Ow, the ball just hit my head.

The ball is slipping through their hands
Hey, be careful of that stand
I'm on again
It's started to rain.

As I slip over my face goes red
The final whistle is blown
I look to find it's the end
We have a victory of 9-3.

Woohoo, woohoo, woohoo!

Hannah Plail (12)
Herne Bay High School

The Wind

I blow and breeze
Sometimes I am harsh
And sometimes I am light
I can grow into storms.

I blow and breeze
I roll the clouds along
I can make you cold
Or just cool you.

I blow and breeze
I can make waves big
Send boats to the seabed
If I am angry.

I blow and breeze
I don't mean to hurt people
It's not my fault
I am misunderstood.

I blow and breeze
I am . . . *the wind!*

Hannah Sheppard (13)
Herne Bay High School

Advertisements

Advertisements through my door
On the TV, what a bore
On the radio, I can't escape
On the bus for goodness sake
They say Coke Zero's the same
But I think it tastes lame
There are 999 channels
All advertising stretchy flannels
They're in the papers, oh my days
Who buys this stuff - anyways!

Callum Mason-Decker (13)
Herne Bay High School

Fish And Chips

Fish and chips
Are tasty when you taste the salt on your lips
Vinegar and brown sauce
Hot, delicious for a nose
Brown paper and plastic cups
Giving you the chance not to wash up.

The shops allow you to take your food away
Instead of eating at a shop, but you still have to pay
Wooden forks and Pukka pies
So tasty you cannot lie.

Fish and chips
Are tasty when you taste the salt on your lips
Vinegar and brown sauce
Hot, delicious for a nose
Brown paper and plastic cups
Giving you the chance not to wash up.

Batter on a sausage
You can eat this at college
Pepper and fizzy drinks
Not as strong as the metal zinc.

Fish and chips
Are tasty when you taste the salt on your lips
Vinegar and brown sauce
Hot, delicious for a nose
Brown paper and plastic cups
Giving you the chance not to wash up.

Anthony Benge (12)
Herne Bay High School

My Big Birthday Surprise

It's my birthday today, *hooray, hooray!*
Oh wait a minute, what's that I see?
A big giant present just for me.

My body temperature keeps rising
My hands keep on shaking
It's too late, I've burst.

Charge! Unwrap, unwrap, says my head
Wait until your family get here, says my heart
Which should I follow? I don't know
Sorry heart, you've got to go!

Undo the bow, be careful, don't break it
Relax my son, the surprise won't last long
Wow! What's next? My special cake!

I've always wanted this, as my mum gives me a kiss
'I love it, I love it, this is what I call bliss.'
'Good,' says Mum, and gives me another kiss!

Charlotte Guilliard (14)
Herne Bay High School

Life

There are lots of different cultures in the world
And some of them mean different things
But we should not be parted on terms of culture.

Countries have rules
But take them too far
Black and white are no different
To who we are.

Why do they think we are so different
Because of the colour of our skin?
We are no different apart from the country we live in.

James Dean (11)
Herne Bay High School

Nan, If Love Was . . .

If love was a giant I would call it my hero
If love was a butterfly I would call it my wings
If love was my space I would call it my freedom
If love was a sandwich I would fill it with peace
If love was my family I would call it my world
If love was my nan I would call it my life.

I could jump off the highest building because I know you will catch me
I could swim across the deepest ocean, because I know you will
keep me afloat
I could run one million miles because I know you will show me the way
I could save my last breath to say 'I love you' because I know you
will do the same
And I will love you forever from this very day.

Nanny, I will never let go, I will always hold on
And I just want you to know you're the one who keeps me so strong.

I would reach up to the mountains, I would shout up to the sky
I would sail the seven seas, I would cherish your very smile
You would lift me if I started falling, you would raise me
if I was down
You taught me right and wrong and you taught me love and peace.

Nan you're the greatest, you're the one who keeps me at bay
You're the one who keeps me living and you're there any time
of the day.

If love was a giant I would call it my hero
If love was a butterfly I would call it my wings
If love was my space I would call it my freedom
If love was a sandwich I would fill it with peace
If love was my family I would call it my world
If love was my nan I would call it my life.

Natasha Savage (14)
Herne Bay High School

The Last Months

I strolled into his house that one fine day
There was my grandad, very joyful I'd say
He had lost all his hair, where had it gone?
I thought it was a joke or maybe a con.

I was aged only seven after all
How could I be such a fool?
He paid for us to go away
To Disneyland, Florida and Flamingo Bay.

Three months later it was March
Above his bed was a handle arch
We had a call that cold, rainy day
I broke down in tears, Grandad had passed away.

I resent cancer, I really do
I hope it never happens to you
It's not fair, no it's not
I miss my grandad *a lot, a lot!*

Megan Catling (12)
Herne Bay High School

Cold And Alone

I can't go back . . .
Not now . . . not ever
No money . . . no food . . . no home
Begging . . .
The only job available
For someone in my situation
'Any change sir? . . . Any change?'

I'm cold . . . I'm hungry
Sitting in a doorway
Their piercing eyes . . . staring at me
They wish I wasn't there
I am a dosser
Alone in the dark
Waiting . . .

Leonie Hopkins (14)
Herne Bay High School

One Word

Forgotten
One word says it best
The heartless souls
They have it all
Alone - it's hard enough.

Forgotten
One word paints the picture
Cold, no feeling in my toes
Hungry, not a morsel passes my lips
Alone - it's hard enough.

Forgotten
One word writes a thousand
No family, no hold, no one
Love, the hole that's not filled
Alone - it's hard enough
Alone - it's hard enough
Alone.

Rebecca Arnold (14)
Herne Bay High School

Am I Dead?

I am a 16-year-old girl
I am homeless
I am sleeping on the streets
Am I dead? Cos this is Hell!

I have no money
I have no food
I have nobody
Am I dead? Cos this is Hell!

Why do people look at me like that?
Why do I feel so empty?
Why does the dark scare me?
Am I dead? Cos this is Hell!

Stacey Norris (14)
Herne Bay High School

This Is Life On The Street

'Got any change man?'
He screwed his nose up.
He then said, 'Have you got any change?'
As he clenched his fist
This is life on the street.

'No, no, no, dude!'
Running in and out of cars
Setting the alarm off on one
This is life on the street.

Sitting in the doorways
Looking at happy people
Raiding bins for food
Sitting in cafés trying to keep warm
This is life on the street.

This is life and this is poor
For people on the streets
This is life on the streets.

Jack Davey (13)
Herne Bay High School

Time Passes By

The stars shining overhead
The sea is glistening in their light
Birds are lying in their beds
It is the dead of night.

I stand and stare at the world around
As time just passes by
There's nothing here, no movement, no sound
Oh how I wish I could fly.

Say goodbye to the moon and hello to the sun
As the stars start to fade away
Today's the day to have some fun
It is the first of May.

Shanon-Kate Woolls (13)
Herne Bay High School

It's Culture Time

It's culture time
It doesn't matter if you're black or white
We're all human beings
It really doesn't matter
Do what you want to do
Eat what you want to eat
Wear what you want to wear
It doesn't matter if you're black or white
All the differences are -
Are the colours of our skins
And where we come from
Afghanistan
England
Spain
Jamaica
It really doesn't matter
It's culture time!

Freddie Mills (11)
Herne Bay High School

Music

Rock, classic, opera or pop
Fast or slow, don't let the beat stop
Music on the airwaves floating all around us
Children with earphones listening on the bus.

Jazz, disco, hip hop and rap
The rhythm hits you, your feet start to tap
Tunes are playing on phones in pockets
Power your stereo with fuel from the sockets.

Country, soul, reggae or blues
Time to put on your dancing shoes
Whatever your style, whatever your taste
Music in life is never a waste.

Bethany Guilliard (11)
Herne Bay High School

I Am

I am a crazy girl who loves to dance
I wonder if I will ever do a dance off
I hear the sound of music pumping in my heart
I see myself dancing with a professional street dancer
I want to be a famous street dancer
I am a crazy girl who loves to dance
I pretend I am the dancing queen
I feel that I will go far with my dancing
I cry when my dancing school is not on
I am a crazy girl who loves to dance
I know in my heart I will get there in life
I say I am the crazy girl who loves to dance
I dream of dancing and one day it will be me
I try to do my best
I hope that I will get somewhere in life
I am a crazy girl who loves to dance!

Shannen Hildred (12)
Herne Bay High School

He Sat There

He sat there, alone and cold
Not a quiver, not a shudder
He sat there, isolated from a careless world
He sat there
In one hand an empty bottle half resting on the ground
He sat there, his body still, hunched over his knees
He sat there, as flames grew and shrank
Lived and died before him
He sat there, the way he always has
He sat there
No more . . .
The cold has gone and taken the hunger too
He is safe from the pain now and forever
He sat there with pursed blue lips and pale skin
He sat there alone, but no longer cold.

Abi Hollingsbee-Pert (14)
Herne Bay High School

I Am

I am a sporty girl who loves dancing
I wonder if I will ever become an amazing dancer
I hear the sound of music
I see fairies dancing in my imagination
I want to carry on dancing when I am older
I am a sporty girl who loves dancing.

I pretend to hold a golden trophy at a dance awards
I feel a glittery dance costume
I touch the silky dance shoes whilst standing underneath
                                    the glistening stars
I cry when I wreck a dance
I am a sporty girl who loves dancing.

I know I am not the best dancer in the world
I say to myself, *try my hardest*
I·dream of dancing at the championships
I try my hardest in every dance I do
I hope to improve at dancing
I am a sporty girl who loves dancing.

Charlotte Hiles (12)
Herne Bay High School

Deep Blue

Watching the sea shining blue
Together we are just me and you.

Blue is the colour of the sky
When I look up it makes me sigh.

Blue is the colour of the sea
Where dolphins swim under to catch the key.

Blue is the glistening, glitter-like ocean
With waves as high as buildings crashing to the sand.

Blue is the colour of dolphins swimming in the sea
They jump and splash about waiting for their tea.

Rebecca Smith (12)
Herne Bay High School

I Am

I am a sporty girl who loves to dance
I wonder if I will ever become a professional dancer
I hear the sound of my dancing school calling my name when
                                                    I'm not there
I see myself in a Hollywood theatre dancing with professionals
                                            and performing solos
I want to become a student at The Royal Ballet School in London
I am a sporty girl who loves to dance.

I pretend that I am in the Royal Albert Hall in London
                        performing ballet, tap and modern dances
I feel the time to improvise when music catches my ears
I touch the softness of the bottom of my dancing shoes
                        when my feet slowly sink into the bottom
I cry with happiness when the judges say, 'You're though.'
I am a sporty girl who loves to dance.

I know that my dancing teachers will help me
                        to achieve the standard they expect me to be
I say to myself every night before I go to sleep,
'I hope I will become a professional dancer, even if I don't
                                            become famous.'
I dream of living in Hollywood and becoming a dancing professional
I try my hardest every time I go dancing to get a higher standard
I hope to meet Anna Pavlova when I am older
I am a sporty girl who loves to dance.

Sophie Collins (11)
Herne Bay High School

Blue

Blue is the colour of sky, blue is the colour of sea
Blue is the colour of my ink pen I use to write my poetry

Blue is the colour of the sky where me and you can just sit or lie
Blue is the colour of the sky where clouds just drift by

Blue is the sea that runs so deep, cold and creepy what lies beneath.

Lucia Wheeler (12)
Herne Bay High School

I Am

I am a loving daughter who loves to shop
I wonder if I'll own my own shop
I hear the sound of my mum's voice and it's music to my ears
I see a massive sale sign saying *70% off*
I want to be a designer
I am a loving daughter who loves to shop.

I pretend I am a model who models clothes for famous people
I feel the warmth of my mum's breath when she leans to kiss me
I touch the moon and stars when I dream
I cry when I hear that baby elephants have died
I am a loving daughter who loves to shop.

I know one day I'll find true love
I say that I have the perfect life
I dream of touching the sky
I hope, I hope to be the best daughter the world has ever seen
I am a loving daughter who loves to shop.

Kerry Maeers (11)
Herne Bay High School

Homeless

H ome is the one thing I want so much but I cannot get
O verlooked by so many people walking by trying to avoid me
M oney, the thing I desperately need but will never be able to grasp
E motional all the time, what else is there to be?
L ife, mine is rotten, I wish it could be better
E ncouragement is what I need to keep going but will never be able

to grasp

S ecurity, I have none, I could be attacked at any time
S ad, it's what I always am, I can never manage to cheer up.

Ben Critchley (13)
Herne Bay High School

I Am

I am a crazy girl who loves horses
I wonder if I'll ever be a professional horse rider
I hear the sound of horses galloping across the field
I see a golden horse waiting for me to ride it
I want to be a horse rider
I am a crazy girl who loves horses.

I pretend to own hundreds of horses
I feel my horse nudging me
I touch my golden horse's mane as we canter along the beach
I cry when horses have to be put down and when they're sad
I am a crazy girl who loves horses.

I know that I will always love and ride horses
I say to all the horses I know 'I love you'
I dream that one day I will own a stable and be an Olympic rider
I try to ride like the best rider
I hope that I will ride in a horse show
I am a crazy girl who loves horses.

Emily Reynolds (11)
Herne Bay High School

The Owl

There was an owl that tu-whit, tu-whoo'd
Good for the owl that tu-whit, tu-whoo'd
He would sit in his tree most of the night
Until he saw a mouse to fight
He swooped down at the brown-coloured mouse
But it ran into a small hut-shaped house
The owl tu-whit, tu-whoo'd as he flew back to his tree
All was quiet apart from a buzz of a late night bee
There was an owl that tu-whit, tu-whoo'd
Good for the owl that tu-whit, tu-whoo'd.

Oliver Whiting (12)
Herne Bay High School

I Am

I am an eagle living on a mountain
I wonder why the strongest people become so weak
I hear the island breeze
I see angelfish in the clear sea
I want to be the first woman on the moon
I am an eagle living on a mountain.

I pretend to be flying and enjoying the scenery
I feel the warm sand on my feet
I touch the baby-blue sea
I cry at romance novels
I am an eagle living on a mountain.

I know fairies use pollen as perfume
I say God is a girl
I dream that I'm a famous designer
I try to cure my mum
I hope to work for Dolce & Gabbana
I am an eagle living on a mountain.

Grace Franklin (11)
Herne Bay High School

We Are One!

Does it matter if someone has different coloured skin?
We are one.
Does it matter if someone is from a different country?
We are one.
Does it matter if they belong to a different religion?
We are one.
Does it matter if they have an accent?
We are one.
No matter what your skin colour is or where you come from
Religion or even accent, we are still one!

Emma Hunter (12)
Herne Bay High School

My School Poem

Getting up at 7am
To get ready for school
Seeing all the older kids
Trying to act cool.

Going into Mentor
Playing with your friends
Having a game of Monopoly
The game never ends.

First period is French
I hate it a lot
Miss always gets stressy
And loses the plot.

After a long day
It's time to go home
Mum's out tomorrow
I'm home alone.

Tia Hills (12)
Herne Bay High School

Fiery Flames

Red is the colour of fire
The hot flames get higher and higher.

Red is the sign of danger
But Jesus is safe away in his manger.

Red is the colour of Rudolph's nose
At this time of year it begins to snow.

Red is the blazing hot, fierce fire
Raging around the forests and killing so new life will form.

Red is the colour of fire at night
It glimmers and shines and gives us light.

Ellie Surridge (11)
Herne Bay High School

Edging Away

The time's edging away
Slowly, ever so slowly
The will's been written
The funeral's Sunday
Why can't they help him?

Why can't I see him?
It's been months
I want to see Nan
How has she coped?

So many die
So many left
To pick up the pieces
Hurry, find us a cure.

Please say it's not true
Tell me he's in the hospital
No, not today
It was going so well.

He's left us now
Don't make me go
To the funeral
Poor old man
But he's elsewhere now.

Ashley Hoskins (12)
Herne Bay High School

Blue Poems

Blue is the colour of the sky
Where we can look as clouds go by.

Blue is the colour of the sky
Where I dream that I can fly.

Blue is the colour of the sea
Where we can sit, just you and me!

Georgina Lambert (12)
Herne Bay High School

I Am

I am a funny girl who likes dogs
I wonder if dogs can talk
I hear dogs barking at the crack of dawn
I see dogs everywhere I go
I want 101 dogs
I am a funny girl who likes dogs.

I pretend that dogs always have puppies
I feel that I should live with puppies and dogs
I touch the smooth fluffy fur
I cry for all of them who pass away
I am a funny girl who likes dogs.

I know that they will be there for me
I say that they care for you
I dream that one day they will talk
I try to keep them company
I hope I can have lots of them
I am a funny girl who likes dogs.

Sarah Kyte (12)
Herne Bay High School

Racism

Why is there racism, we are all the same?
It doesn't matter whether you are black or white
Tall or short, fat or thin
We all live together in this world and we should all get along
We all have family and somebody to love
We are all the same and it's a shame that some people don't know that
When you're walking down the street and somebody calls you a name
Because of your race and it makes you feel so small
All I want to know is why, why is there racism?

Victoria Lawrence (12)
Herne Bay High School

I Am . . .

I am funny and sporty
I wonder if me and my friends will bring peace to the world
I hear a giant chocolate monster
I hear a dog barking in excitement
I see a dog smiling whilst watching Mauresmo play a fantastic shot
I want to be a teacher or a famous tennis player
I am funny and sporty.

I pretend that I'm holding the golden, intricate-patterned tennis racket
With my name engraved in italic writing
I feel the beat of the tennis balls hitting my racket like balls of hot,
                                                        flaming fire
I touch the leather-beaded collar belonging to the silky-furred,
chocolate Labrador puppy
I cry when I fall and hurt myself
I am funny and sporty.

I know that me and my friends will be friends forever
I say, 'Fetch, good boy,' to my dog
I dream of being a teacher, a good one at that
I try to be more active and alert whilst playing tennis
I hope that me and my friends will be friends forever
I am funny and sporty.

Mollie Eyles (11)
Herne Bay High School

Culture

C hoose to explore new ways of living
U nderstanding other religions
L ook beyond the colour of a person's skin
T o be open to other people's way of life
U nderstanding cultural differences in society
R ealise that everyone is different
E veryone is entitled to have their own religious beliefs.

Jake Heddershaw (12)
Herne Bay High School

I Am . . .

I am an Arsenal fan and I love to watch them play football
I wonder if I'll see Arsenal play again
I hear the Arsenal fans cheer when Arsenal score a goal
I see Theo Walcott score a smashing goal
I want to see Arsenal play at their new stadium the 'Emirates'
I am an Arsenal fan and I love to watch them play football.

I pretend that I play for Arsenal and score loads of goals
I feel like when I play football I'm Thierry Henry
I touch a piece of an amazing pitch
I cry when Arsenal lose to rubbish football teams
I am an Arsenal fan who loves to watch them play football.

I know I will watch them play football again
I say Arsenal are the best football team in the universe
I dream that I played at the 'Emirates'
And when I ran out of the tunnel there was a tingle down my spine
I try to play the way Arsenal play beautiful football
I hope Arsenal will beat Chelsea and Man U 12-0
I am an Arsenal fan who loves to watch them play football.

Adam Ford (12)
Herne Bay High School

Culture

Culture is all around us, it's everywhere we go
It's what the world's made up of
It's how we live and go
Every country has its different little thing
We eat our different food, we look our different looks
But it doesn't matter because we are all human
We have our different religions but that's who we are
All this horrible stuff should stop because we're all human.

Ashley Nevard (11)
Herne Bay High School

I Am . . .

I am a mad nutter who loves football
I wonder whether I will become a football player for West Ham
I hear a roaring crowd singing my name
I see myself playing in the FA Cup final for West Ham at Wembley
I want to play for West Ham
I am a mad nutter who loves football.

I pretend to play for West Ham
I feel my teammates congratulating me
I touch the ball as I pick the ball out of the net to carry on with the game quickly
I cry when West Ham get relegated
I am a mad nutter who loves football.

I know Alan Curbishley can keep West Ham up
I say West Ham will stay up
I dream of playing for West Ham
I try to achieve all of my goals
I hope I will eventually play for West Ham
I am a mad nutter who loves football.

Matt Radley (12)
Herne Bay High School

Imagine A Culture

Imagine a culture with black and white race
Imagine a culture with love and no hate
Imagine a culture where what you wear makes no difference
Whether it be a sari, jeans or filigrees
Imagine a culture with fish, chips and curry
Imagine a culture with no reason to hurry.

Sarah McCracken (11)
Herne Bay High School

I Am . . .

I am a musical girl who loves dancing
I wonder whether you can dance with two left feet
I hear my feet tapping along the corridor
I see myself dancing on stage with Missy Elliot
I want to dance with professionals
I am a musical girl who loves dancing.

I pretend I'm a professional dancer
I feel my soul leave my body when I dance
I touch my toes during a dance move
I cry when I make a mistake
I am a musical girl who loves dancing.

I know I might not fulfil all my dreams
I say give me a chance
I dream of being a professional at my hobbies
I try to make my dance moves original
I am a musical girl who loves dancing.

Chenelle Williams (12)
Herne Bay High School

Blue

Blue is the colour of the sky
It also happens to be the colour of my eyes.

Blue is the colour of a blueberry
And it's not for you, it's for me.

Blue is the colour of the sea
That makes you need a pee.

Ryan Cubbage (11)
Herne Bay High School

I Am . . .

I am a madman who loves dogs
I wonder if dogs could stand upright
I hear them begging me to feed them
I see cats and dogs getting on with each other
I want to have a hundred dogs in my house
I am a madman who loves dogs.

I pretend to smile when a dog bites me
I feel sad when dogs pass away
I sing along as I run with my dogs
I cry when I leave my dogs all alone when I go on holidays
I am a madman who loves dogs.

I know when dogs feel lonely
I say every dog is equal
I dream about them every day
I try my best to train my dogs to the best of my ability
I hope to be a dog trainer when I'm older
I am a madman who loves dogs.

Jason Chow (12)
Herne Bay High School

Red Is The Colour

Red is the colour of a rose
And it has thorns that hurt my nose.

Red is the colour of a berry
Which is another type of sweet cherry.

Red is the colour of my car
It drives me near and far.

Luke Corrigan (12)
Herne Bay High School

I Am . . .

I am a weird person who loves football
I wonder, will a car go 2,000mph one day?
I hear music in my ears
I see a football match going on
I want to be a footballer
I am a weird person who loves football.

I pretend to be a famous footballer
I feel I'm floating in the air
I touch everything in creation
I cry when important things go wrong
I am a weird person who loves football.

I know my mum and dad want me to do well at school
I say school is quite fun
I dream of owning a mansion one day
I try to work hard all day
I hope that Chelsea FC win the UEFA Champions League one day
I am a weird person who loves football.

Sam Sinclair (12)
Herne Bay High School

Red

Red means anger, red means hot
Red is the colour of my cooking pot
Red is the colour of roses
And their scent flows up your noses
Red is the colour of the rose
That smells quite nice under my nose
Red is the colour of blood
Also red is the colour of love.

Katie Packman (12)
Herne Bay High School

I Am . . .

I am a crazy girl who loves to shop
I wonder, I wonder if I'll ever become a designer
I hear the sound of clothes saying, *'Buy me!'*
I see a huge sign saying *Buy me*
I want to be a designer
I am a crazy girl that loves to shop.

I pretend I am walking down a red carpet with a silver sparkly dress on
I feel the texture of the material in my hands
I touch other clothes made by Ted Baker
I cry when shops don't have my size
I am a crazy girl that loves to shop.

I know that I will *always* love shopping
I say to myself every night, 'Will I ever become a designer?'
I dream of modelling a silver diamond dress
I try to think that I am in a cloud of clothes
I hope I will meet the person that makes Dolce & Gabbana clothes
I am a crazy girl that loves to shop.

Nadia Commentucci (12)
Herne Bay High School

Blue Is The Colour Of . . .

Blue is the colour of the bright sky
Where birds fly ever so high
Blue is the colour of the splashing waves
Venturing deeper into the undersea caves
Blue is the colour of the sea
When I look in, there's a reflection of me.

Abigail Heard (11)
Herne Bay High School

My Family

If my family went, I don't know what I'd do
They have been with me through and through
They taught me how to walk
And they taught me how to talk
If I have a problem, they will help me
Because, you see, they're my family.

They gave me clothes and food
And they listened when I was in a mood
My sister is always there
Because she really cares
My grandad, mum and dad are in my family
Don't forget Rosie, my little baby.

Rosie is three
Ten years younger than me
My sister is fifteen
She is sometimes very mean
I love her really
And all of my family.

In case you didn't know, Rosie is a dog
You can barely see her in all of the fog
My dog Rosie
Is very, very nosy
So now you see
They're my family.

I say all of this and I love them
Because, you see, they're my family.

Katie Gurney (13)
Herne Bay High School

I Am . . .

I am a strange monkey man who loves guinea pigs
I wonder if guinea pigs can drive little cars
I hear wise old guinea pigs talking
I see monkey zombies
I want a pet that can do supernatural things
I am a strange monkey man who loves guinea pigs.

I pretend that I am a racer
I feel faster than the speed of light
I touch a high speed motorbike
I cry when I get hurt
I am a strange monkey man who loves guinea pigs.

I know evil never wins
I say stop all wars
I dream of being a fantasy warrior
I try to achieve my goals
I hope to live a good life
I am a strange monkey man who loves guinea pigs.

Ben Hughes (11)
Herne Bay High School

Red Is The Colour Of . . .

Red is the colour of the Devil's daughter
Waiting patiently for the chance to slaughter
Red is the colour of stop on a traffic light
Used against darker colours, it is very bright
Red is the colour of the poster on the wall
Which some kids say is really quite cool.

Kerrie Anderson (12)
Herne Bay High School

Mixed Race

I, the one who is mixed
Our fate decided, our future fixed
I'm the one who ate rice and beans
They are the ones to eat haute cuisine
We are mixed
They're the ones to have a car
But we are the ones to walk far
They're the ones to have heating
But we are the ones who got beaten
They are treated very differently
But we are treated with suspicious minds
Because we are mixed
That's how it feels to be treated
When we are mixed race
So get used to it
See what I mean
We are no different
Everyone of us, a human being!

Thomas Wickens (12)
Herne Bay High School

Losing You!

She has gone, she has gone
But where to?
I didn't even get to say goodbye
But to who?

How do I know if she still cares?
I wonder if she's safe
Remembering all the good times we shared
Did she believe in faith?

She wasn't there, she wasn't there
How do I know if she'll come?
I loved her warm feel when she gave me a hug
How will she cope, how will my mum?

Clare Bates (13)
Herne Bay High School

Old People Smell

Old people smell
Old people can't tell
When their teeth have fallen out.

They lie all day drinking tea
And watching TV.

When you come back
They lie on their back
And say, 'I've been here all day!'

You make them tea
You switch on the TV
But still there's no thank you.

I hate looking after my nan
Next time I'm staying in the van.

Lauren Snoad (13)
Herne Bay High School

The Rose!

The rose glistens in the sun
It's as colourful as sweets
Innocent as children.

As red as a beating heart
A handful of love
As swift as gentle summer air.

Prickly as a hedgehog
Sweet as a candy bar
Red like the sun on a beautiful day.

It feels like velvet
Smells like perfume
As beautiful as birth.

Give me a rose
And show me your love.

Tanya Stevens (12)
King Ethelbert School

An Unforgettable Nightmare

I walk down into this dead city
Dragging my feet through the dusty street
Blood stained into black ash and dust
As my hands start to tremble
I can hear the screams inside my head
A memory remains
I can hear the deafening ring of screams.

The red grass bears the flesh of young children
And playgrounds explode under their feet
In an inferno rush of bright light and heat
Young screams and infants' painful tears;
Echoes of people dying in the streets.

The innocent die young on the fields
They will never last;
Just a memory will remain -
A skin-burning scar no one can ever forget
The city's features burn and twist before my eyes;
An impact on my life
A scar on my eyes
An unforgettable nightmare.

Craig Barsby (15)
King Ethelbert School

Snake Poem

The purple rough snake slithers
Flicking its yellow forked tongue
It coils its rattle tail
Then swiftly raises its head
Preparing to strike at its prey
Leaving it to rot in the sunshine.

Shane Gonesh (12)
King Ethelbert School

Vampire

Gliding through the night
Soaring and flying
Preying on unexpected victims
Watching them fall asleep
Creeping in their rooms
Feeling their blood pulsate throughout their body
One bite . . . one small bite . . .
A small gasp of pain
Then motionless
Blood dripping from the lips
The taste, oh the sweet taste
Sweet, yet salty
The victim pants as if out of breath
Pupils large and full
Blood draining from their face
A new assistant to the Count
Another member of the death-dealers awakened
Another vampire unveiled.

Lauren Harris (15)
King Ethelbert School

Roses

Rose petals dance swiftly in the air
And land on the ground delicately
With passion and innocence
As elegant as they look.

No matter what they do or say
They still have the heart of an angel
The colour of love
As beautiful as birth.

Ebony Barkes (12)
King Ethelbert School

What Is Love?

What is love?
Love is unbelievable
Love is unforgettable
Love is incredible
Love is special
Love is love.

What is love?
Love that natural high
When you feel you're floating in the sky
Love is going under the cover
That's how you become a mother
Love is a kiss or a hug
It's so warm like hot cocoa in a mug.

What is love?
Love is amazing, it's so powerful and so strong
It can last a second or a lifetime long
Love can make you happy but can also make you sad
Love can be a good feeling or it can be bad.

No one really knows what love is . . .
But it always waits for us, it never goes away once it's found
It's in your heart moving around
It remains somewhere deep inside
So no one knows your feeling, they just hide.

Love could be anything, any shape or size
You don't have to see it with your eyes
Love is infectious, you can catch it like the flu
When someone loves you, you automatically love them too.

What is love?
Love is unbelievable
Love is unforgettable
Love is incredible
Love is special
Love is love.

Emma Baggus (14)
King Ethelbert School

Roses

Roses, roses, they are so sweet
People buy you them for a treat
What you do with them, it's up to you
But put them in a vase, please do!

Roses, roses, they smell so fresh
The thorns on them may get in your flesh
They sway in the breeze
With the rhythm of the trees!

Roses, roses, red, yellow, white and pink
When you put them in water they don't sink
They stand proud and posh
When you drop them in water, they go *splosh!*

Roses, roses, they represent love
They look peaceful just like a dove
It's nice to receive them on a special day
And to receive them in a special way.

Roses, roses, their petals are like silk
Don't put them in a vase of milk
When they start to wilt, they are going to die
When they do that, you'll give a big sigh!

Emma Kerr (13)
King Ethelbert School

Dolphins

Dolphins swim and dive
Ocean waves tumble
Playful, powerful somersaults
Splashing and streamlined
Fins and tails dive
In and out of waves
Dolphins play and splash all day.

Emily Jeffries (12)
King Ethelbert School

Untitled

It makes you feel welcome and warm inside
If you're worried you can speak to a teacher, you don't have to hide
You get to go on school trips, to many different places
Everyone loves King Ethelbert's, I have never seen so many happy
faces
You learn a new thing every day
When it gets to 3.20pm, you just want to stay
You can stay in the LRC if you have work to do
It makes you feel proud walking around in navy blue
There are many after school clubs, where you can have fun
If you're athletic, you will love the annual run
The canteen's great, with lovely food
It will cheer you up if you're in a mood
Walking around with a crown on your chest
Everyone knows *KES* is the best!

Franchesca Onken (12)
King Ethelbert School

The Ancient Forest

The forest is cold and heartless
It keeps your secrets safe and sound
It keeps them safe all year round
Birds conspiring like little spies
It wheezes and whistles like an old man
It's sweet in the night, busy in the day
It's stiff and fragile like a china plate
In winter the forest sleeps in a blanket of leaves and snow.

Joshua Lee (13)
King Ethelbert School

A Dog's Life

A dog likes to play with his toys
A dog licks me when he misses me at work
He misses me until I come home and give him love.

Their names are Max and Patch
My pet dogs, they are my boys, they love to run
They wag their tails to show me they are Man's best friend
They like food to eat and sometimes they eat my food.

When I was watching the telly about dogs
Patch and Max climbed up the telly
Patch was bad because he jumped over the wall.

I like my dogs because they are loveable boys
And I love Patch and Max, my dogs.

Carl Harris (15)
St Anthony's School, Margate

Anaconda's Features

Anacondas want to hunt
And are up to 40 feet long
It stalks its prey
It opens its mouth wide to 180 degrees
It has a colour vision eyesight
It creeps up to its prey
Kills its prey tight till it's dead
It hides in shallow or deep waters and also in bushes
It also sleeps with its eyes open
It holds tight onto its prey for twenty to thirty seconds or minutes
Other predators try to hunt it without noticing it
It normally hunts at night and is very strong
Some people have it as a pet
It lives for 30 to 40 years.

Robert Reynolds (15)
St Anthony's School, Margate

Old Codger

There was an old codger from Blackpool
Who was a really silly old fool
He sat on his hat,
He slid on the mat
And hit himself with a rigid hard tool.

Bret Linsdell (14)
St Anthony's School, Margate

One

You can only have one person
Who's really kind and true
No other friend in the whole wide world
Will be the same as you.

As I look upon your picture
The sweetest memories I recall
And a face full of joy and happiness
And a smile for one and all.

Dear Jesus take this message
To our good friend up above
Let him know we miss him
And give him all our love.

Your life was love and kindness
Your love for your friends true
You did your best for all of us
And we will always love you.

You gave life to others
And yet yours was stolen away
But I just keep dreaming
That I'll be with you some day.

Jonathan & Michael Hanly (18)
St Edmund's Catholic School, Dover

Why?

What is the point?
Why are we here?
The meaning of life
Is not so clear.

The reason for living
A question not explained
I want to know the answer
Someone should complain.

So why do we exist?
Is there an explanation?
The reason for being
It'll shock the nation.

Daniel Sims (15)
St Edmund's Catholic School, Dover

Thinking Of Home

I am a soldier sitting in a trench
Thinking of my wife and my kids
And happy times in a park with a bench
But now we are pawns on a chessboard grid.

Thinking of happy times gone by
Swallows and sparrows kissing the sky
Now six feet under ice-cold earth
As weak and helpless as they were at birth.

A whistle blows us over the top
And rapidly our numbers start to drop
Bullets whip left, right and overhead
Then one of them finds its mark
And one of us is dead
And for one of us the world is dark.

Tim Benfield (12)
Simon Langton Boys' School

If I Could Travel . . .

If I could travel . . .
I would lie on a white sandy beach
The sun on my back beating down like a golden beach ball
If I could travel . . .
I would stand and feel the cascading water of the falls crashing down
like howling clouds
If I could travel . . .
I would gaze from ice-capped mountains, floating flakes all around me
Now so numb that the thick snow felt like no more than cotton candy
If I could travel . . .
The Amazon I would explore, a tropical wilderness, on all fours
Playing with friendly vipers, meek lambs in my eyes
If I could travel . . .
I would gallop through the woods on a beautiful black stallion
Dive in the deep salty seas alongside beautiful dolphins
If I could travel . . .
I would visit a tropical paradise known only to me
Exotic birds twittering around me, playful foxes inches away
If I could travel . . .
I would meander through the desert on the hump of a camel basking
in the radiant sunlight
But no, I am confined to my gilded cage, trapped here in my
little caravan.

Anna Chadwick (11)
Tonbridge Grammar School

Dreams

I wake up from a long, long sleep
With thoughts and wishes from the deep
Swirls of colour enter my eyes
Though nothing seems to be a surprise
Magic and mystery stuck in my mind
For my dreams were filled with everything combined.

Wonderful dreams, wonderful dreams!

It feels so false and yet so true
All these messages out of the blue
I love my dreams for they give me pleasure
So now I keep them for an eternal treasure
When I sleep a sudden glow of fun
The story opens up for it has only just begun.

Wonderful dreams, wonderful dreams!

Pretty, everlasting flowers
All kinds of creatures with magical powers
Pixies, elves and fairies too
Smile and laugh and play with you
I take off and begin to fly
Soaring and swooping through the sky.

Wonderful dreams, wonderful dreams!

Every night another story
Sometimes bringing triumphant glory
I am rather sad as the day draws near
But now I know there is nothing to fear
I can daydream throughout the day
No . . . what would my teachers say
So now I keep my dreams for the night
When I am snug in my bed and tucked up tight.

Wonderful dreams, wonderful dreams!

Mari Shirley (11)
Tonbridge Grammar School

The Empty Art Classroom

After a lesson
I stay behind
With no other person
But I don't mind.

At a paint-spattered table
I am myself
Only here am I able
Not anywhere else.

In my wonderful dreams
I'm a great artist
I create on all themes
With a flick of my wrist.

Whilst smelling the paint
From the Year 7 display
I patiently wait
For a great future day.

In my dreams I am famous
My paintings are rare
My sketches are countless
My portraits are fair.

The curtains are flappy
Where I sit alone
And yet I am happy
Up there, on my own.

Far away a bell's ringing
It drags me away
But my heart is still singing
From my treat of the day!

Charlotte Whittaker (12)
Tonbridge Grammar School

Bunnies

Watch him jump
The furry lump
Tiny nose
He'll smell a rose
Your thumping
Jumping bunny.

Watch him hop
Up to the top
He's so fluffy
Not like Buffy
Your thumping
Jumping bunny.

He can walk
While you talk
He's so fat
Like a cat
Your thumping
Jumping bunny.

You might have a baby bunny
He probably acts very funny
He has a fluffy tail
It's good he can't wail
Your thumping
Jumping bunny.

He has floppy ears
Glad he can't shed tears
Give him cuddles
While we jump over puddles
Your thumping
Jumping bunny.

Rachel Hannah (11)
Tonbridge Grammar School

Water

An emerald-green glass
Tang of earth and grass
My eye is caught by distortion
The ripple-echo of a skating ghost
Still, calm, flowing, tumbling water.

A dancing, tinkling sprite
Gurgling onwards with all its might
My ears are filled with roaring
The rainbow-flash of a hillward fish
Still, calm, flowing, tumbling water.

A sparkling veil-like wall
In an endless, slow-motion fall
I feel the pull of the torrent
Can barely resist its roar
Still, calm, flowing, tumbling water.

Deep blue with infinite power
Crashing endlessly under salty winds
The warm turquoise waters lulling me to sleep
I dream of creatures finning through the deep
Still, calm, flowing, tumbling water.

Alice Hill (11)
Tonbridge Grammar School

The Forest At Night

The forest at night is a gruesome place
With shadows dancing in front of my face
Eyes watching me, where can I run?
No means of light, no lamp, no sun.

Leaves crunching beneath my feet
I feel my heart as it skips a beat
My eyes dashing all around
Where is that thing? What was that sound?

Trees hanging like washing to dry
Will I survive or will I die?
My knees feeling cold and weak
Then I hear a sudden screech.

The knife plunges through my heart
It feels just like a poison dart
My life will never be the same
For I will never live again.

Because the forest at night
Is a gruesome place.

Amie Humphrey (12)
Tonbridge Grammar School

Autumn

Winter is coming, summer has gone
Autumn is here and here to belong
Gone are the holidays along with the fun
Now school time has finally begun
Before the leaves were full and green
Now colours of red and gold can be seen
The leaves are falling to the ground
When walked over they crackle their sound
Leaving trees empty and bare
On them nothing for which to care
Dying leaves on the ground
Only their skeletons can be found
Wind is rustling through the trees
Creating for me a gentle breeze
Winter is coming, summer has gone
Autumn is here and here to belong.

Rebecca Fox (11)
Tonbridge Grammar School

Flanders Field

In Flanders Field the poppies grow
People come and people go
In Flanders Field
Eagles fly high
In the sky.
In Flanders Field
Families read their telegrams with a silent hush
In Flanders Field
The sun is not shining and the sea is not blue
I am really missing you.

Amy-Jane Greenwood (12)
Tonbridge Grammar School

The Great War

They gave their lives for us, these men
We will always remember them.

Bullets ring out in the frosty air
Mercy and pity in this bloodbath is rare.
Bravery and courage, shells and grenades,
They fight like warriors in great crusades.

News of the soldiers arrives home at dawn,
For those who died, their families mourn.
Lost fathers, sons and brothers,
Lamenting sisters, daughters and mothers.

Long after the battle is fought and done,
From the horizon comes the sun.
Blood-red poppies in Flanders field,
From war comes nature's scarlet yield.

They gave their lives for us, these men
We will always remember them.

Megan Beddoe (11)
Tonbridge Grammar School

Night

Out in the dark you hear a dog bark
You turn and you run away.
The trees sway around you whilst you hope and pray
That nothing jumps out of the night.
The fright that you feel is let loose in a scream
As you slowly turn around.
The ground underneath you is soggy and wet
Then you hear the sound.
Your heart pounds as the sound gets closer and closer.

The night is a scary place, a dark and dismal place.
You hope and pray that nothing jumps out of the night.

Laura Morrison (11)
Tonbridge Grammar School

Disaster!

Crash, bang!
Smash, wham!

What was that?
All I heard was a smack.

Blood dripping from my wounds
The blood oozing and dark maroon.

Pain was killing me
I couldn't even see the car that had hit me.

Beep, beep went the life-support machine
I couldn't believe it, I was only 16.

The thought of the crash made my head smash!
Silence struck the air and all I can remember is . . .
Crash, bang!
Smash, wham!

Eleanor Horswill (11)
Tonbridge Grammar School

My Cat

My cat is fat and lazy
He has gorgeous green eyes and soft grey fur
This just makes him purr.
My cat is fat and lazy
He eats an awful lot
Almost as much as an ocelot.
My cat is fat and lazy
He always gets in the way
Ignoring everything I say!
My cat is fat and lazy
He spends so much time on my bed
You would think he was dead!
My cat is fat and lazy
Even though all these things are true
I love my cat, I really do!

Samantha Stephenson (12)
Tonbridge Grammar School

My Dog

When I wake up in the morning
He's in his cosy bed
In his cosy bed
When I walk across the kitchen
He lifts his sleepy head
Lifts his sleepy head.

As I open up his dog crate
He stretches, then leaps out,
Stretches, then leaps out
He rushes round the downstairs rooms
To see who is about
To see who is about.

He watches out for breakfast time
He listens for the door
Listens for the door
He knows that if there's food around
He must sit down on the floor
Must sit down on the floor.

His bright black eyes are fixed on me
His feathery tail flicks wildly
Feathery tail flicks wildly
His pink tongue flickers in and out
He lifts his small paw mildly
Lifts his small paw mildly.

The food is guzzled rapidly
No time to waste today
No time to waste today
He needs to track his favourite toy
And find someone to play
Find someone to play.

Joanna Barnett (12)
Tonbridge Grammar School

Deep Within The Sea

Every pebble tells a story
Just like you and me
Every pebble has grown from a grain of sand
Deep within the sea.

Every wave lives
Just like you and me
Every wave begins
Deep within the sea.

Every grain of sand is needed
Just like you and me
Every grain of sand has a home
Deep within the sea.

Every rock is strong and steady
Just like you and me
Every rock will end up
Deep within the sea.

So will the rest of the world
You and me
Thanks to global warming, we'll all end up
Deep within the sea.

Emma Keywood (12)
Tonbridge Grammar School

Dream Box

I put my dreams into a box,
So they will not spoil.
I put my dreams into a box,
Underneath the soil.

If future generations,
Want to come and have a look,
They will see me learn to fly
Even see me catching rooks.

All my dreams are kept inside,
Even those I wish to hide.
Climbing up a mountain,
Walking on the moon.
Discovering a fountain
And when it snowed in June.

But all my nasty dreams
All my foul nightmares
Are pushed down to the bottom,
Should anyone get scared.

I put my dreams into a box,
I hope somebody finds it.
I put my dreams into a box,
But what if they don't like it?

Emma Beale (12)
Tonbridge Grammar School

Climate Change

Ice melting
Temperature's sweltering
Seasons changing
Less rain raining

Everything is different

Winters warmer
Summers too
Humans way of life changing
Almost like new

All this fuss, but who to blame?
Politicians hang their heads in shame
Celebrities smile as they talk to the news
At least it will be sunnier in the UK too

Yesterday's world battles with today
Suffering polar bears in the Arctic they lay
Rainforests being chopped down force monkeys to leave their homes
Children sigh as there is no chance of snow

Powerless
Loneliness
What is there to do?
To do?
To do?

Alice Matthews (11)
Tonbridge Grammar School

Let's Go Down To The Beach

Let's go down to the beach
And pick limpets
One each!
We'll have them for tea
Just you and me!
Oh, do let's go down to the beach!

Let's go down to the beach
We'll climb the rocks
That's if you can reach!
So we can see the view
Maybe even have a picture or two!
Oh, do let's go down to the beach!

Let's go down to the beach
And swim in the sea
Don't worry - I can teach!
We can dive off the rocks
Still dressed in our socks!
Oh, do let's go down to the beach!

Let's go down to the beach
Have a picnic
With an apple or a peach!
We'll lie on the sand
Hand in hand!
Oh, do let's go down to the beach!

Alex St Clair (12)
Tonbridge Grammar School

Tears You Cry

(Own adaption following inspiration from Gollum's song at the end of 'Lord of the Rings - The Two Towers'. Original lyrics by Fran Walsh)

In the end, I'll be what I will be
No loyal friend was ever there for me
And don't say goodbye to me
The waves of time fade away from me

These tears you cry are falling rain
Of all the hurt you told them
The hurt, the blame

Of all the things that you didn't do
Only one could ever come from you
And I say that's very true
But I say we still need you

These tears you cry are falling rain
Of all the hurt you told us
The hurt, the blame

Yet in the end, I'll be what I will be
No loyal friends were ever there for me
The waves of time fade away from me
And don't say you didn't try

These tears you cry are falling rain
Of all the lies you told us
The hurt, the blame.

Tilly Leeper (12)
Tonbridge Grammar School

The Woods

In the woods, burning bright
In the middle of the night
Burning eyes peeping out
Followed by a weasel's snout.

In the woods, burning bright
In the middle of the night
Owl's swooping very low
Is it friend or is it foe?

In the woods, burning bright
In the middle of the night
The milk-glass moon sat
No ear can hear the echo-locating bat.

In the woods, burning bright
In the middle of the night
Fox cubs romp and play
As the vixen stalks her prey.

In the woods, burning bright
In the middle of the night
Digging away is the mole
Burrowing yet another hole.

In the dawn of first light
Birds chorus their delight
The nocturnal animals say goodnight
Turning their backs on the emerging light.

Martha Jesson (11)
Tonbridge Grammar School

Zombie

If you're a zombie and you're feeling peckish
You come from behind and go for the neckish
Suck out the brains
. . . brains
. . . brains
Grey blood in your veins
Just the body remains
Your soul in chains.

If you're a zombie and you look in the mirror
Your empty eye sockets could be a lot clearer
But you can make out a figure, getting closer, getting queerer
. . . queerer
. . . queerer
Twisted grin
Skeletally thin
Trapped within.

If you're a zombie and the spell starts to fade
You *explode* everywhere like a shaken lemonade
For a second your spirit is no longer afraid
, , , afraid
. . . afraid
One last roar
Then here no more
Grey goo on the floor
RIP.

Jasmine Vorley (12)
Tonbridge Grammar School

Lick, Lick, Lick

Lick, lick, lick,
Cocoa, eggs,
'Let me have some,'
My sister begs.

Lick, lick, slurp,
In my house cake is a fixture,
Flour and sugar,
Go into the mixture.

Lick, slurp, munch,
Chocolate slice, lemon slice,
All these crumbs,
Left for the mice.

Munch, munch, munch,
'But wait!'
My sister cries,
'Where is the cake?
Tell me no lies!'

I stay quiet.

Jemima Silver (12)
Tonbridge Grammar School

Love

Love is a smile
Love is a wish
Love is a hug
Love is a kiss.

Love can mean anything
Love can be everything
Love is a feeling
When you are dreaming.

Love is a flower
Love is a heart
Love is power
Love can take you apart.

Love is beyond your dreams
Love is a memory in your mind
Love isn't all it seems
Love is something you can find
Love is something you can find.

Lydia Hamblet (11)
Tonbridge Grammar School

I Love You . . .

The colours blur and sway
Whispering as if to say
I love you . . .

The sun slips away
A dancing figure in the sky
Whispering as if to say
I love you . . .

It is dark now as I lay
Under the stars of night
But no one is here to hear me say
I love you.

Katie Pembroke (12)
Tonbridge Grammar School

The Dream

I am like a piece of driftwood
In a sea of unconnected thoughts
Swirling, diving and bobbing . . .
The line of courtiers bow before me
And hail me, their English queen.
I stride majestically towards the stone walls
And see above me the parapets and portcullis
But is this Windsor?
The walls are lined with Trojan soldiers
Their armour gleaming, swords flashing
Glinting in the Mediterranean sunshine.
I am now marching towards the walls of Troy,
A shout rises behind me,
'Achilles, Achilles, Achilles!'
I am bellowing the name of my cousin's killer,
Ready to avenge his brutal death.
'Hector, you coward! Come and fight me!' I shout
I run towards him as he emerges
Dashing, charging, running . . .
And now I am on a track.
Nearing a bend in a group of runners, my competitors.
I hear the roar of the crowd.
'Kelly, Kelly, Kelly!' - I find the extra power.
The surge. The turbo boost. The acceleration.
Open track in front of me, the finish approaching
I dip my head and charge through the invisible barrier of glory.
Rushing, diving, falling.
Not the Queen. Not Achilles. Not Kelly Holmes.
I awake. Alone.

Alexandra Baddeley (12)
Walthamstow Hall School

Young Writers Information

We hope you have enjoyed reading this book - and that you will continue to enjoy it in the coming years.

If you like reading and writing poetry drop us a line, or give us a call, and we'll send you a free information pack.

Alternatively if you would like to order further copies of this book or any of our other titles, then please give us a call or log onto our website at www.youngwriters.co.uk

Young Writers Information
Remus House
Coltsfoot Drive
Peterborough
PE2 9JX

(01733) 890066